ON TO GLORY!

THE INSIDE STORY OF WALES' 2019 GRAND SLAM TRIUMPH

Published under license by Vision Sports Publishing Limited

Welsh Rugby Union Limited
Principality Stadium
Westgate Street
Cardiff
CF10 1NS
www.wru.co.uk

Vision Sports Publishing Limited
19-23 High Street
Kingston upon Thames
Surrey
KT1 1LL
www.visionsp.co.uk

ISBN: 9781909534971

Editors:	Toby Trotman, Luke Broadley
Text:	Alex Bywater
Design:	David Hicks Design
Photography:	Huw Evans Agency
Other photography:	Getty Images; Wales players'/coaches' own
Statistics:	Guinness Six Nations official website

Printed in Slovakia by Neografia

GRANDSLAM
CHAMPIONS 2019

ON TO GLORY!

THE INSIDE STORY OF WALES' 2019 GRAND SLAM TRIUMPH

VSP

"Winning the Grand Slam was special for the players, but it was special for Warren Gatland too as it was his last tournament as head coach. He's been pretty prolific not just with Wales, but with the British & Irish Lions as well. I don't want to be too romantic about it, but when you have someone who is so confident at the top of the tree, that filters down and it's hard to ignore."

DRIVING THE PACK

The Wales captain explains exactly what it takes to be the leader of a proud nation and to win a Guinness Six Nations Grand Slam

I'm very fortunate in what I get to do. I've been Wales captain for a while now. It's not something I ever aspired to, but I'm very proud on every occasion I'm given the opportunity to lead the team. It's a pretty special job.

To be captain of your country when you win a Six Nations Grand Slam is something which is definitely up there with all I've achieved in the past. It's a validation of all the hard work we do. A lot of people don't actually realise how much work it takes and the highlight of it for me was being able to share the Grand Slam moment with my two daughters on the pitch. I'll always remember it for that, more than anything. You don't realise about those sorts of things when you're younger, but family is what it's all about for me now.

When I look back on lifting the trophy, I wish it could have lasted a little bit longer. When you're at the centre of it all, it feels like a moment where if you blink, you'll miss it! I've been lucky enough to win a Grand Slam a couple of times before and you just want to take it all in – you want to make the most of it. It was nice to share the moment with Jonathan Davies, with him lifting the Triple Crown. It was important that the whole team was there and the only downside when I look back on it was that the roof was open. It meant everyone got a bit wet, but I say that tongue-in-cheek – if I'm honest. It's important you don't waste those moments and I just hope we'll get more opportunities to have similar days in the future. I include myself in that and hopefully they're not too far away. The Six Nations tournament grows as a competition year-on-year and got even more competitive again in 2019.

This tournament had more significance because we have the World Cup coming up and people are trying to work out seedings and rankings. We didn't go into it looking at that, but we did have confidence from a decent run of nine wins. It all started in the last game of the 2018 Six Nations where plenty of changes were made. A lot of guys were given an opportunity and when you combine that with the fact that many others were given a chance in Argentina and in the autumn, we were in a pretty decent place. There was still a lot of work for us to do, but to win the Grand Slam and in the manner in

> **"A lot of people don't actually realise how much work it takes and the highlight of it for me was being able to share the Grand Slam moment with my two daughters on the pitch."**

which we did it, was fantastic.

We were pleased with what we achieved last autumn in gaining a first clean sweep. I wouldn't use the term 'monkey off the back' when referring to our November win over Australia because I think that's far too basic. We have been very close against teams from the southern hemisphere – and particularly Australia – in years gone by. We are well aware we still have to face them at the World Cup. The autumn was a junction where we all came together, we all performed well, and we built on the start of the year we'd made, which was really important. We had a big pool of players and everyone got an opportunity. Other players were rested at certain points.

That put us in good stead for the Guinness Six Nations tournament. When we looked at our run of fixtures we knew that we would be doing the Six Nations a disservice as a competition if we discounted France, Scotland and Italy. Despite Italy's results, they are improving – if you look at what they are actually doing both domestically and internationally – they are getting better.

They are always due a big performance and as an opposition player, you just don't know when that is going to come. France are a very dangerous side. It's the same for Scotland with the way they've been playing in the last 12 months. They are one of the most surprising teams in the tier one bracket. England and Ireland →

→ are always going to be up there because they win a lot of games, but we didn't have any specific focus on either of them before the tournament. It's a cliché I know, but it was definitely one game at a time for us and a case of building on the performances we'd already had. That's why it was pleasing to continue the momentum we had in previous campaigns into the Six Nations. We won the Grand Slam, but we're also very real about the fact there are things for us to improve on in our game. That will always be the case and we have to make sure we're aware of it. We were 16-0 down at half-time in the first game against France and we were 16 points to the better at half-time in the last game with Ireland. There is a level of consistency there we can work on.

At the end of the day captaincy is just a label and on basic terms I count myself as a member of the team, just like any other. That said, I've been pleased to see the development of the younger players alongside our senior guys. We have a very strong leadership group – Ken Owens and Jonathan Davies are experienced players now and play a key role, but people often forget guys like Gareth Anscombe, Cory Hill, and Adam Beard who has really stepped up. Adam calls the line-outs a lot of the time and is maturing by the day. Dan Biggar is another one, and perhaps he didn't start as many games as he would have wanted. He was still at the forefront of everything we do as a senior leadership group. We don't have to applaud anyone for taking on responsibility or making important decisions. All the players do it and from a captaincy point of view, all that co-ordination makes dealing with the squad a whole lot easier. It's everyone's job to lead, not just mine. A lot of the young guys have taken the opportunities they had in Argentina last summer when others were rested. Opportunity can be a very fleeting thing, and sometimes people get one, but don't take advantage.

Josh Adams in particular has been one of our star performers. He's been coming on game-by-game and learning really well from George North.

"Hopefully we can continue to make Wales as a country proud and give you, as supporters, more to cheer about. Thank you for all your support. You have no idea how much it means to us."

Maybe it's easier at a younger age now, but these guys are leading themselves and each other. I don't have to tell them what needs to be done. I'm just really proud for such a small nation that Wales is able to produce players like that. Proud is the right word and we just try to show that on the field. It's very simple. Winning the Grand Slam was special for the players, and for Warren Gatland too, as it was his last tournament as head coach. He's been pretty prolific not just with

Wales, but with the British & Irish Lions as well. I don't want to be too romantic about it, but when you have someone who is so confident at the top of the tree, that filters down and it's hard to ignore. Warren has a bit left on his contract so he can't take his foot off the gas yet, but his record with three Grand Slams speaks for itself.

I was very flattered to be named Player Of The Championship. To be up there as a nominee with three other Welsh players and two outstanding players from England would have been more than enough and I'm very grateful to the people who took the time to vote.

We enjoyed the celebrations after the Ireland game. The men I played with as a younger player set standards and that's what I still try to do today. In the Ireland match I wanted to produce a performance which justified the occasion, but that's not just me, it's the same for the whole team and coaching staff.

I hope you enjoy this book and reading some insight from other players and coaches on the 2019 Guinness Six Nations. It was a great championship for us, but at the same time it is now very clear in all our heads that it has gone. Now we've got to reassess, look at where we're at, and seek to improve again.

We'll have the chance to have some time away from the game in the next few months and it's important that we use it wisely because it's going to be a long journey for those who are selected for the World Cup in Japan. Hopefully, we'll have most of our players back available, because guys who have needed operations have had them now.

I said after the Grand Slam win we've now put a target on our backs, but we have to be comfortable with the pressure that comes with that. If we do drop a game, it won't be panic stations, we will regroup and go again because we have a very mentally strong squad. Hopefully we can continue to make Wales proud and give you, as supporters, more to cheer about. Thank you for all your support.

You have no idea how much it means to us. ∎

It takes a team on-and-off
the field to be successful

LAYING THE FOUNDATIONS

Autumn, 2018

"When people look back at the 2019 Guinness Six Nations and the Grand Slam, they will think of the months of February and March. Our journey to that success actually began in September 2018. It was at that point we decided that for the four games in the autumn series we were going to train and work the boys much harder than normal."

PAUL 'BOBBY' STRIDGEON

The four victories in the November Under Armour Series provided a crucial platform for the 2019 Grand Slam. The 9-6 win over Australia was particularly significant, as a late Dan Biggar penalty saw Wales secure their first victory over the Wallabies in a decade

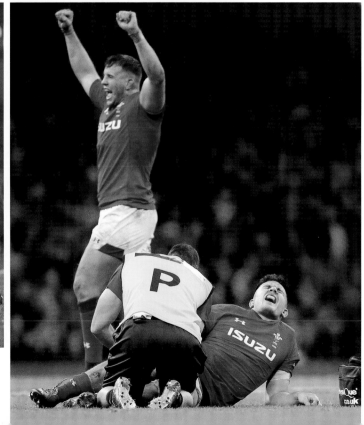

BOBBY STRIDGEON

The Wales management team are the unsung heroes of the Grand Slam. Paul 'Bobby' Stridgeon, the team's Head of Physical Performance takes you behind the scenes into the engine room

What most people see is the glory. They watch the matches, they see us lift the trophies, and they even see me running around Principality Stadium taking selfies in the rain! The things they don't see are the planning, the relentless training the players have to do to get ready for Test rugby, and all the hours put in by the coaches and backroom staff. It's all worth it.

When people look back at the 2019 Guinness Six Nations and the Grand Slam, they will think of the months of February and March. Our journey to that success actually began in September 2018. It was at that point we decided that for the four games in the autumn series we were going to train and work the boys much harder than normal. We knew if we made some big fitness gains in those four weeks we could carry it through to the Six Nations and it would give us a better chance of winning it. In a normal campaign you work hard in the fallow weeks and then taper it for match weeks, but in the autumn we worked very hard in the first fallow week and very hard in the build-up to Scotland which was our first game. It meant we were in a good place to play Australia. We saw November as a fitness period for us, but to work the boys as hard as we did fitness wise, still win all four games, and get our first November clean sweep was absolutely brilliant. We had our cake and ate it.

To get positive results against Scotland, Australia, Tonga and South Africa meant we extended our winning run to nine matches. We want to win every game we play in, but at that time the big focus and long-term goal was on fitness, winning the Six Nations, and making us better for the World Cup.

We did a lot of conditioning and small-sided games including touch rugby. We did what we call a Bronco test. That is where the players run from zero to 20 metres and back, zero to 40 and back, and zero to 60 metres and back. That's just one rep and they do five in a row. It's tough. It's non-stop. We also do a lot of power endurance stuff where the boys are wrestling, pushing a weighted prowler, pulling a weighted sled, or sprinting. It's 15 seconds on, 15 seconds off, and we do that about eight times.

We got a lot of hard conditioning in and in the autumn we even did it on a Thursday when that would normally be a pure rugby session. It meant we started the Six Nations from a better point

> **"With the lads we have in this Wales squad there are absolutely no egos. It's hard graft, but they just get on with it. It's the best squad I've ever been involved in."**

than we have done in the past and we were brutal on the players in the first week. We looked after them for the first few days after they came out of European rugby, but after that we killed them again. We really put them in a hole. There is no other way of putting it, with the lads we have in this Wales squad there are absolutely no egos. It's hard graft, but they just get on with it.

This is the best squad I've ever been involved in and I've been in a few. We take the players to a place that's not very nice, but they shake my hand at the end of every session and say thanks even if they've been vomiting! The fallow week before the England game was the hardest we have ever worked. It was brutal because we hadn't performed as well as we wanted to against Italy and Warren Gatland was a bit perturbed. The sessions were horrible. Whenever someone dropped the ball the boys all did what we call a 'Hennie Muller'. They start on the halfway line, they run diagonally across to the try line, then they run the length of the try line along the in-goal and then diagonally across to the other bit of the halfway line and then back to the start. Basically it's a lap of half the pitch in a Union Jack formation. That was really, really tough. It was just brutal for the boys and a lot of them were definitely sick after that. That's the sort of place you have to go to if you want to be ready for Test rugby. Those are a couple of examples of what the players go through and it's something the →

The Wigan lads together
– Shaun Edwards with
another crucial member of
the team, Paul Stridgeon

WHEN IN ROME...

"The boys trained very hard throughout the Six Nations, but some of them were given extra motivation when we were in the hotel gym in Rome before the Italy game. We rotated the side for that match and during the week I took a few of the guys who weren't in the starting side or were on the bench down for a work-out. Who did we bump into there? Only Dolph Lundgren! He's a massive actor and played Ivan Drago in the Rocky films. He was huge in Rocky IV as Balboa's rival and the boys loved it! Alun Wyn Jones was on the bench for the Italy game so he was down there. Rob Evans and Ken Owens were too. They were all star struck and behaved like little boys around him! We had a few selfies in the gym with him and he even did a few weights with us. He was there working on a film and was in the same hotel for seven weeks. I'm sure he would have lifted heavier weights than some of the lads back in the day, but he's a bit older now and was just ticking over. He was great to chat to and his presence definitely made the boys work harder in the gym that day!"

→ public don't see. It is all part of the plan put together by Warren, the coaching staff, and the back-room team. The team we have has been together for a long time now. We know each other inside out. It all works seamlessly and the key for me is Gats has people around him he can trust. Shaun Edwards and I have spoken a lot about this. We all know roughly what Gats wants and he lets us get on with it. We are all one team. Warren is the top dog, but we have Rob Howley, Shaun, Robin McBryde and Neil Jenkins who all play vital roles. Everyone we have in our set-up is world class at their role and that goes for the coaches, the medics and doctors, the analysts, strength and conditioning, and fitness team. We're all in it together and the 2019 Six Nations was no different. We all get on so well and that's important. There is a lot of autonomy with Gats and not much micro managing. We do have disagreements, but we're all mates and as soon as we come to an agreement, everyone buys into it. That's brilliant, really. We don't have a lot of meetings. We all eat together as a staff the night before a game and leave the players to eat in the team room. On a Monday night in camp we all meet for a quick beer to talk things through because Tuesday is generally the week's big day. Gats gets the best out of all of us and one thing he is big on is family. He always says it's the most important thing and it is. If anyone has any problems we're urged to tell Gats and then it can be sorted out. At the last Rugby World Cup we had one player whose partner was struggling a bit with a new baby.

He asked Gats if he could go back to Wales from London on our day off, but Gats said you don't have to drive and he booked an extra room in the team hotel for his partner and little one. That player stayed in his room with his team-mate, but it meant he could visit his family as they were 100 metres away! That to me sums up the team spirit and togetherness we have in our camp. We're in a good place on and off the field after the Guinness Six Nations. In international

"Warren is the top dog, but we have Rob, Shaun, Robin and Neil, who all play vital roles. Everyone we have in our set-up is world class at their role."

rugby you do need a bit of luck with injuries, but my view is a lot of that is down to good management. Unfortunately, we had one contact injury in November with Ellis Jenkins, but that was in a match and not training. We do give our players good management. Our injury rate has been good recently and what we have is a very integrated performance team. The boys monitor themselves every day in terms of how they've slept, how they're feeling, and all sorts of other things.

All that detail goes into an iPad and we know if anyone isn't feeling right. We can then follow it up. We use GPS data to monitor the players' workload and we know what each player should be doing. If that's too high, then we may pull that player out of a session. The fitness, medical, and strength and conditioning teams are all involved in that. Warren doesn't mind if we trim training down by 15 or 20 minutes if needed. We're not on the training field for hours. Everything is intense, the coaches are switched on, and a 70-minute

session would be a long one for us. It's about concentration and keeping the boys fresh. You can't keep beasting the players all the time. There is a time and a place for everything. That takes me back to the selfies! That's how I celebrated us winning the Grand Slam after the Ireland game. It was an amazing few days. If you'd told me we'd win it when we were 16-0 down at half-time in the first game in France I wouldn't have believed you. Prince William is always a big face around our celebrations. Rob Evans was running around with his top off in the changing room, he was soaking wet from the Ireland game, and he kept saying to the Prince 'Let's have a selfie!' He kept grabbing him and going 'Come on, mate!' I was thinking 'Oh my God' and I wondered what was going through Prince William's head. We all had a good drink afterwards and met up with the players on the Sunday as well. Prince William is such a good guy and very down to earth. He was awesome with the boys, just brilliant. He never turned down a picture. The celebrations lasted a few days and we've now won our last 14 games. As a coaching group we've looked at changing little things to keep the boys fresh and we have done subtle bits and bobs, but nothing major. Winning keeps the boys fresh. The boys know what is coming in each campaign and there are no surprises. They know they're not just being thrown the latest fad. That will be the same for Rugby World Cup.

I just can't wait. I've already begun working on the Rugby World Cup plan. Huw Bennett (assistant strength and conditioning coach) is the same. He texted me pretty soon after to say how much he's looking forward to it. We just want to get into it now. We could equal New Zealand and England's record winning streak of 18 matches if we win our four warm-up matches, but that won't be our focus. It's about making sure we're ready for Japan. After the last 18 months we've had, I can't tell you how excited I am about it all and as a coaching group it would be the perfect way to say goodbye. ■

Left: Paul Stridgeon on the touchline about to celebrate the win over Ireland, and in the dressing room with the trophies and HRH Prince William, The Duke of Cambridge, who is the Welsh Rugby Union Patron and a loyal supporter of the team

The players were stretched and tested in the squad's training camps like never before as the management team exhausted every avenue to deliver the country a Guinness Six Nations Grand Slam

FRANCE V WALES

Friday 1st February, 2019

"Time stood still... I knew he only had two options – take it straight up the middle or throw a long pass. He chose to pass. Then everything just slowed down. It was weird. All I could think was 'Oh my God, he's passed it'. I watched it the whole way, I picked his pass off, and as soon as the ball was in my hands, I knew no one was going to catch me."

GEORGE NORTH ON THE MOMENT THAT KINDLED WALES' GRAND SLAM HOPES

Left: Gareth Anscombe gets in the groove before the kicking duties begin against France

Bottom left: Tomas Francis had a huge task on his hands against the impressive France scrum

Above: Josh Adams gets ready for the aerial onslaught Wales were expecting on a wet night in Paris

Far left: While warming up George North could have had no idea how big his role would be against France

Left: Alun Wyn Jones faces the world's media as the Guinness Six Nations kicked off on a Friday night in Paris

An expectant crowd of 60,000 awaits the start of the 2019 Guinness Six Nations

GEORGE NORTH

The Ospreys wing recounts one of the most remarkable matches in his illustrious career and a moment no Wales fan will ever forget

Time stood still. I saw it a mile off. Sébastien Vahaamahina picked the ball up in midfield and I knew he only had two options – take it straight up the middle or throw a long pass.

He chose to pass. At that point in the game France had kicked a lot, our defence was out of shape, and I knew that whatever I did next, I couldn't repeat the mistake I'd made earlier in the game that had led to a try for France.

Then everything just slowed down. It was weird. All I could think was 'Oh my God, he's passed it'. I watched it the whole way, I picked his pass off, and as soon as the ball was in my hands, I knew no one was going to catch me.

I couldn't think as I ran clear, but as soon as I put the ball down I had a brief moment to enjoy myself. I knew then we were in a good place. We had turned it around.

My 36th try for Wales meant we had come back from 16-0 down to win in Paris. We didn't know it at the time, but it was a Six Nations record for the biggest comeback. It was a great start to our campaign.

We got the job done in the end, but we also knew we'd got ourselves out of jail. The match in Paris was very much a game of two halves, both for us as a team and me personally.

On the back of an unbeaten November campaign we went into the Guinness Six Nations with confidence. In the weeks before the France game the coaches made us work

so hard in training and it paid off in Paris. The boys were out on their feet in training and gasping for air it was that bad.

Warren Gatland says he and the coaches will never apologise for working us hard. It was almost like a mini pre-season in terms of getting us ready for the intensity of what was to come in the Six Nations.

International rugby is always a huge step up. You need to have Test match fitness in your lungs and legs because if you go into a game cold, you will suffer. You won't be able to cope.

The fitness work we'd done in training meant we were in a good place physically, but the other positive thing to come out of it was the development of our mental strength. That was shown in the France game. We knew we were fit enough to play for 80 minutes and get the win.

As starts go though, we were caught cold. We had prepared well in the weeks prior to the game, but we were all quite shocked at how bad the weather was. We knew it would be bad, but not that bad. The conditions were awful with driving rain and we just didn't get started.

France scored through Louis Picamoles and Yoann Huget and Camille Lopez kicked a penalty and a drop goal. We were lucky Morgan Parra missed a couple of shots at goal as well. At half-time no one →

PHOTO: GETTY IMAGES

"As starts go though, we were caught cold. We had prepared well in the weeks prior to the game, but we were all quite shocked at how bad the weather was. We knew it would be bad, but not that bad. The conditions were awful with driving rain and we just didn't get started."

George North goes through his final preparations before taking on France

needed to say anything. We already knew we were playing nowhere near our full potential. It felt like we hadn't had the rub of the green either. People often think that in those sorts of situations the coaches speak magical words to us about what it means to represent Wales and the history of the players who have played in the shirt before.

That does happen, but in France it was actually the exact opposite. Everything was very calm and very straight to the point. I'm sure everyone out there has had their parents say to them 'I'm not angry, I'm just disappointed' or something similar at some point or other.

It was very much like that in Paris.

Those exact words weren't actually said, but that was the insinuation and it made me feel horrendous. We knew we weren't doing what the coaches had trusted us to do.

There is no worse feeling.

Losing as a Wales fan is awful, but as a player I can't even begin to tell you how horrible it is. When rugby is as big as it is in our country, you want to do the whole nation proud.

We didn't do that in the first 40 minutes in Paris. The half-time message from Warren and the coaches was not to panic. They told us to put the ball in the right areas of the field. They told us if we built pressure on France they would crumble. The main message was - we had to front up.

The whole stadium knew the first half was not what Wales can produce as a team, so we came out for the second half and we were straight back on our mettle. I knew I had nothing to lose. In the first half I'd made a bad defensive mistake which allowed Huget to score. I set myself high standards and was disappointed with my error. I was determined I had to put things right.

We managed to put France under pressure at the start of the second half and we started to see some cracks open up. Josh Adams made a great break for Tomos Williams' try. That started it all off. It showed the pressure

France were under and from there we knew we had to keep turning the screw. Our second try saw my game come full circle. All week we had spoken about how the conditions would impact the game and how it would be difficult to pick the ball up in wet weather.

Hadleigh Parkes – who is not renowned for his kicking – hoofed it down field and nine times out of 10 you chase that sort of kick and the player will clear. This time was the exception to the rule. I'd decided at half-time I was going to empty the tank and chase everything knowing we only had 40 minutes to put things right. That's why I ran hell for leather after Hadleigh's kick. Fortunately for me and unfortunately for Huget, he slipped and spilled the ball. If you ever want to see a moment where your world can change in a split second, that was it. It was huge for both of us, but for different reasons. I'll never turn a try down, even if that one was from half a metre. They all count.

Now we had the momentum. Lopez kicked a penalty, but when Vahaamahina threw his long pass I managed to race away for my second and we held out at the other end.

Before the game Warren had said if we beat France in the first game, we'd win the Six Nations. It was very typical of Gats' style. As soon as he said that the pressure fell straight on our shoulders. Whack!

We'd heard about it all week from the media. At half-time I don't think that was in anyone's

"I'd decided at half time I was going to empty the tank and chase everything knowing we only had 40 minutes to put things right. That's why I ran hell for leather after Hadleigh's kick."

thoughts, but after the game Warren said 'That was a close call, wasn't it?'

We'd let large parts of the game get out of our control and had left it far too late for our liking. Warren told us if we let another team have a 16-point head start, we'd never win the Grand Slam. Our comeback in France showed me the strength of leadership we have in the squad and also how tight we are as a group. What Warren has instilled in us over the years is a very non-Welsh mentality. The Welsh way is to be very quiet and as a nation we're sometimes scared to say how good we are. We're always under the radar and in someone else's shadow.

But what Gats has instilled in us is to have the confidence to back ourselves in our ability to close games out. Sometimes that involves winning ugly like in France. It's not arrogance, but we have belief in ourselves that regardless of what anyone else says, we can go out and win. If you don't believe in yourself, no one else is going to.

We all knew we had a lot to work on after France. Even though we had won, the mood had already turned to Italy. It was such a late match in Paris that we didn't get to the after-match function till 1am. We got lost in the Stade de France on the way there! What should have been a two-minute walk ended up taking 25 minutes. We were all dressed up in our suits and had no idea where we were going. We made it eventually, but it was a weird 24 hours. We played a game, won, got lost, and then had to be up only a few hours later for a flight to Nice where we were training ahead of the Italy match. On the way there I was sat next to Ross Moriarty who fell asleep on me. He doesn't snore, but he has a really heavy head and I wondered what I'd done to deserve that. Maybe it was some sort of punishment for my defensive blunder!

We were all absolutely knackered that Saturday morning, but while we'd got lost in the Stade de France, we knew our Grand Slam bid was on the right path. There was still more to come. ■

Although Josh Navidi helped Wales to their seventh win in eight matches against Les Bleus – it was France who dominated a hard-fought first half in Paris

France shot into a 16-0 lead... but Wales showed grit, determination and belief to overcome the huge deficit

Left: France were in the driving seat before being shackled by Wales as the red tide turned

Above: The rain fell on Warren Gatland and his Wales team but the head coach never lost faith in his players

Above: Josh Adams turned in an accomplished display including the crucial break that allowed Tomos Williams to give Wales some hope

Right: Williams slides over at the start of the second half and what had seemed impossible, became possible

The ball slips from the grasp of Yoann Huget...

... Wales wing George North pounces...

... and one of the most unlikely comebacks in Championship history is on!

George North wasn't content with one try, picking off a pass to sprint home from 50 metres as Wales leapt off the canvas

The boys can hardly believe that North has done it and laid the foundation for an opening day victory for Wales

FRANCE 19 24 WALES

Date Friday 1st February 2019. KO: 8pm **Venue** Stade de France, Paris **Referee** Wayne Barnes (England) **Attendance** 60,000

15 Liam Williams (**10** Gareth Anscombe 66')
14 George North (Man of the Match)
13 Jonathan Davies
12 Hadleigh Parkes (**23** Owen Watkin 77')
11 Josh Adams
10 Gareth Anscombe (**22** Dan Biggar 53')
9 Tomos Williams (**21** Gareth Davies 53')
8 Ross Moriarty
7 Justin Tipuric
6 Josh Navidi (**20** Aaron Wainwright 78')
5 Alun Wyn Jones (Captain)
4 Adam Beard (**19** Cory Hill 48')
3 Tomas Francis (**18** Samson Lee 57')
2 Ken Owens (**16** Elliot Dee 73')
1 Rob Evans (**17** Wyn Jones 73')

15 Maxime Médard
14 Damian Penaud (**22** Gaël Fickou, 63')
13 Romain Ntamack
12 Wesley Fofana (**23** Geoffrey Doumayrou 67')
11 Yoann Huget
10 Camille Lopez
9 Morgan Parra (**21** Baptiste Serin 58')
8 Louis Picamoles (**20** Grégory Alldritt 71')
7 Arthur Itturia
6 Wenceslas Lauret
5 Paul Willemse (**19** Félix Lambey 58')
4 Sébastien Vahaamahina
3 Uini Atonio (**18** Demba Bamba 48')
2 Guilhem Guirado (Captain) (**16** Julien Marchand 58')
1 Jefferson Poirot (**17** Dany Priso 61')

Tries (3): T Williams 47', North 52', 72'
Conversions (3): Anscombe 48', 53', Biggar 73'
Penalty: Biggar 62'

Tries (2): Picamoles 6', Huget 24'
Penalties (2): Lopez 33', 70'
Drop goal (1): Lopez 41'

Scores

5-0, Picamoles try; **10-0,** Huget try; **13-0,** Lopez pen; **16-0,** Lopez drop; **16-5,** T Williams try; **16-7,** Anscombe con; **16-12,** North try; **16-14,** Anscombe con; **16-17,** Biggar pen; **19-17,** Lopez pen; **19-22,** North try; **19-24,** Biggar con.

SIX NATIONS 2019: ROUND 1

TEAM	PL	W	D	L	PF	PA	DIFF	TF	TA	BP	PTS
Scotland	1	1	0	0	33	20	13	5	3	1	5
England	1	1	0	0	32	20	12	4	2	1	5
Wales	1	1	0	0	24	19	5	3	2	0	4
France	1	0	0	1	19	24	-5	2	3	1	1
Ireland	1	0	0	1	20	32	-12	2	4	0	0
Italy	1	0	0	1	20	33	-13	3	5	0	0

> **"What Gats has instilled in us is to have the confidence to back ourselves in our ability to close games out. Sometimes that involves winning ugly like in France. It's not arrogance, but we have belief in ourselves that regardless of what anyone else says, we can go out and win."**
> GEORGE NORTH

Above and Right: Hadleigh Parkes celebrates a famous win while Jonathan Davies shows full respect to his French opponents

Left: The team reflect on one of the greatest comebacks rugby has ever seen

THE BREAKDOWN

16
Wales came from 16-0 down at half time to win in Paris. **No team** had ever overturned such a big deficit in Six Nations history.

19
George North's two tries at the Stade de France took him to a total of 19 for Wales in the Six Nations.

20
The number of successful tackles made by **Justin Tipuric** and **Ross Moriarty** against Les Bleus.

95
Metres carried by full-back **Liam Williams**, who had a first-half try ruled out.

62
The minute Wales took the lead for the first time through **Dan Biggar**'s penalty.

Above and Left: Back in the away dressing room the Wales team reflect on a victory at the start of the 2019 Guinness Six Nations campaign

ITALY V WALES

Saturday 9th February, 2019

"A lot of people will be writing us off, which is a good place to be in and hopefully we can just come in under the radar. I thought Italy played exceptionally well. They looked to play some rugby and created a couple of opportunities. They're a tough team to break down here in Rome and for me that's probably the best Italian performance I've seen since I've been in charge."

WARREN GATLAND

Wales took the unusual decision to spend the week before the Italy Test in Nice, where they headed after Paris. It gave the team the chance to test themselves in a different environment and while they enjoyed some 'down time' the coaches ensured they were put through a lot of hard work on the French coast

Left: Wales fans travelled in big numbers to watch their heroes match their best-ever run of 11 straight Test wins, set in 1910

Bottom left: Jonathan Davies earned the honour of captaining Wales, for the first time. He was one of just five Welshmen to keep their starting place from the win over France

The Stadio Olimpico was the perfect setting for this Guinness Six Nations match, with a crowd of 38,700 in Rome

JOSH ADAMS

A much-changed Wales side arrived in Rome but they still emerged victorious, Josh Adams scoring one of his team's two tries against Italy

52

A lot of guys got a chance to impress in Rome and although I wouldn't say we had the complete performance, it was a better and improved performance and we won a little more comfortably, than against France a week earlier.

The victory against Italy also meant we equalled the Welsh record of 11 wins in a row which dated back more than 100 years. I was proud to be a part of that, but as a team we didn't talk too much about it. No matter who you play against, it is always difficult to win away in the Guinness Six Nations and that's why the mood in the camp was positive after the match. To come out of the France game with a 'W' was massive, especially given the way we played in the first half in Paris.

Jonathan Davies was captain for the first time. He was pretty cool, calm, and collected as usual. When you make 10 changes to a team there are certain things you have to get used to and it can take time for the team's game to click.

"As a wing when you're in a try-scoring mood, you just want them to keep coming. That's what happened to me in this Six Nations."

For example, when the centre pairing changes it's important as a winger like me that you adapt to what goes on inside you. Different players pass and kick at different times and take on different angles of running. Maybe we hadn't got used to each other as quickly as we would have liked to in the first half, but it was much better in the second. I managed to get over for a key try and I didn't have to do much.

The rest of the lads in the back line did all the work. I remember Thomas Young was at scrum-half for some reason, Owen Watkin and Foxy – that's what we call Jonathan Davies – both touched the ball and then Liam Williams handed off his defender and hit the gap. He was tackled just short of the line, but thankfully I was in support to sprint over. It started a pretty good run for me of three tries in three games as I went on to score against England and Scotland too. As a wing when you're in a try-scoring mood, you just want them to keep coming. That's what happened to me in this Six Nations.

Italy gave it everything and never went away, but Owen got his first try for Wales from a Gareth Anscombe chip and that gave us a bit of a lead. It was one we held on to.

After the game we knew we had a rest week to follow, but there was no danger of us partying or going on a mad one. My girlfriend Georgia is a school teacher so she was working on the Friday and unfortunately, she was unable to get out to

Right: Adams celebrates another win for Wales and a try for the Worcester Warriors flyer

→

→ the game in Rome on the Saturday. It was too difficult, but her parents Alec and Leanne were over and they came to the team hotel after the match. We had a big room there where all the players relaxed with their wives, girlfriends and families and that's how we spent the evening. It was a shame Georgia wasn't there, but it was nice for her parents to be a part of it.

I'll always remember the week before the Italy game. Why? I'll have to be honest and say it was because of the chicken wings. Oh, and George North's Chocolate Buttons! Delicious! The build-up to the match in Rome was certainly unusual because after the win over France in round one we flew to Nice for a training camp rather than returning home to Wales. It was obviously very different and a change in environment for us, but with both of our first two games of the campaign being away from home it was a chance to mix things up a bit.

It made sense to stay away and as a group we loved the idea. It was a great chance to work hard on the field and bond together as a squad off it. There was a lot of chicken eaten that week! About two blocks away from our hotel in Nice there was a Hard Rock Cafe. The boys spent a lot of time in there and the chicken wings were very popular. I won't name names, all I'll say is we were very good customers.

We were all looking forward to Nice, but when we arrived on the Saturday it was absolutely pouring down. We couldn't believe it. The weather eventually improved and we had a great week. We trained at Nice Rugby Club. The thinking behind the camp was to make sure we were well prepared for the World Cup. When we're in Japan later this year we won't be based in the same place all the time and we'll have to use different players at different stages of the tournament. The build-up to the Italy week was a good way of preparing for that. We took 31 players for the nine or 10-day period we were away and that was again what we can expect at the World Cup where we will have the same sized squad.

We all got a bit of sun on our backs which put the boys in a really good mood. We did our recovery in the sea just outside the hotel instead of the usual ice bath. One thing I can say for sure was that Nice definitely wasn't like the wet, cold and wind of Wales!

We had a day off on the Wednesday and a few of the lads went across to Monaco. When I have a day off I try and stay off my feet as much as possible, so I just had a quick look around Nice city centre. Some players like a coffee on their day off and to relax and talk about stuff outside of rugby. That's what I did. Others were different and Liam and a few of the other boys went over to Monaco, and when they came back all they could talk about were the cars, boats and yachts they had seen there. Most of the lads realised all that stuff is a bit above our pay grade, but there were some who came back dreaming that they might own something like that one day. Again, I won't mention any names!

When we were allowed some time away from rugby we enjoyed our new surroundings, but the coaches made sure we didn't feel like we were on holiday. There was no chance of that. After the comeback win in France the mood in the camp was pretty good. I roomed with George for most of the Guinness Six Nations. He's just a great bloke, one of the best I've come across in rugby.

> **"The thinking behind the camp was to make sure we were well prepared for the World Cup. In Japan later this year we won't be based in the same place all the time and we'll have to use different players at different stages of the tournament."**

It helps that we play in the same position so we have a lot in common there and he has really taken me under his wing since I've been involved in the senior Wales squad.

For a young player like me to be able to pick his brains on certain things is only going to help me improve and I'm very lucky to have him there as a sounding board. What he has achieved in his Test career with all those caps at the age of 27 is just amazing. If I can get anywhere close to that I'll be delighted.

The other great thing about having George as a roommate is he always provides the sweets on the night before the game. He delivered the goods in Rome. Normally we have some Haribo and a bit of chocolate, but before the Italy game we had special large Chocolate Buttons. Good work, George!

We had flown to Rome from Nice straight after training and doing some media on the Thursday afternoon. We had lived the dream for a few days, but now the focus was fully on business. Warren Gatland made 10 changes for the game. I was delighted to still be in the side. It gave me a lot of confidence. The coaches did a very good job that week in keeping us grounded, working us hard, and telling us we had to be on our toes ready for a tough battle with Italy. They ended up being spot on.

The win was good for the confidence of the squad. We always knew that with England coming next in Cardiff the level was going to go up. We had meetings before the Six Nations started and we had full belief from day one that our squad was good enough and we were well-coached and well-drilled enough to go on and win the championship. We didn't think about the Grand Slam because you always take each game as it comes and you never want to look too far ahead. We were two from two, but at the same time we also knew England were the form team after beating Ireland in Dublin.

A huge occasion was around the corner in Cardiff. We all knew it was going to be a big one, but at least we had two weeks to prepare for it. ∎

The team celebrates Adams' 54th minute try, Wales' first in Rome and one which set them on course for victory

Left: Aled Davies runs into the blue Italian wall

Above: Dan Biggar was as reliable as ever from the tee, kicking 14 points against the Italians

Above: Josh Navidi turned in a world-class performance to be named man of the match

Right: Liam Williams provided a strong foundation, making a decisive break for the first try

Josh Adams sprints to the line for Wales' first try

Above: Thomas Young got his chance – proving the strength in depth in the Wales squad – although he suffered agony late on when a try was disallowed

Left: Owen Watkin grabbed his first try for his country – in the 70th minute – to round off an accomplished performance

Below: Jonah Holmes gained more metres (98) than any other Welshman in Rome, justifying his call-up to the side and Six Nations debut

Ross Moriarty whispers sweet nothings in the ear of his back-row colleague Thomas Young after a job well done for Wales in Rome

ITALY 15 26 WALES

Date Saturday 9th February 2019. KO: 16.45 **Venue** Stadio Olimpico, Rome **Referee** Mathieu Raynal (France) **Attendance** 38,700

15 Jayden Hayward	**15** Liam Williams (**23** Hallam Amos 67')
14 Edoardo Padovani	**14** Jonah Holmes
13 Michele Campagnaro	**13** Jonathan Davies (Captain)
12 Luca Morisi	**12** Owen Watkin
11 Angelo Esposito	**11** Josh Adams
10 Tommaso Allan (**22** Ian McInley 48'-54')	**10** Dan Biggar (**22** Gareth Anscombe 55')
9 Guglielmo Palazzani (**21** Edoardo Gori 60')	**9** Aled Davies (**21** Gareth Davies 63')
8 Sergio Parisse (Captain)	**8** **Josh Navidi** (Man of the Match) (**20** Ross Moriarty 67')
7 Abraham Jurgens Steyn	**7** Thomas Young
6 Sebastian Negri (**20** Marco Barbini 57')	**6** Aaron Wainwright
5 Dean Budd (**19** Federico Ruzza 52')	**5** Adam Beard
4 David Sisi	**4** Jake Ball (**19** Alun Wyn Jones 51')
3 Simone Ferrari (**18** Tiziano Pasquali 60')	**3** Samson Lee (**18** Dillon Lewis 51')
2 Leonardo Ghiraldini (**16** Luca Bigi 60')	**2** Elliot Dee (**16** Ryan Elias 67')
1 Nicola Quaglio (**17** Cherif Traorè 51')	**1** Nicky Smith (**17** Wyn Jones 63')
Tries (2): Steyn 34', Padovani 75'	**Tries (2):** Adams 54', Watkin 70'
Conversion: Allan 36'	**Conversions (2):** Biggar 55', Anscombe 71'
Penalty: Allan 44'	**Penalties (4):** Biggar 2', 15', 19', 30'

Scores
0-3, Biggar pen; **0-6,** Biggar pen; **0-9,** Biggar pen; **0-12,** Biggar pen; **5-12,** Steyn try; **7-12,** Allan con; **10-12,** Allan pen;
10-17, Adams try; **10-19,** Biggar con; **10-24,** Watkin try; **10-26,** Anscombe con; **15-26,** Padovani try.

SIX NATIONS 2019: ROUND 2

TEAM	PL	W	D	L	PF	PA	DIFF	TF	TA	BP	PTS
England	2	2	0	0	76	28	48	10	3	2	10
Wales	2	2	0	0	50	34	16	5	4	0	8
Scotland	2	1	0	1	46	42	4	6	6	1	5
Ireland	2	1	0	1	42	45	-3	5	5	0	4
France	2	0	0	2	27	68	-41	3	9	1	1
Italy	2	0	0	2	35	59	-24	5	7	0	0

THE BREAKDOWN

11
Wales' win in Italy made it 11 in a row which equalled a **Welsh rugby record** dating back to between 1907 and 1910.

99
Percentage of rucks where **Wales** retained their own ball.

98
Metres carried by Wales wing **Jonah Holmes**, the most of any Wales player.

10
Number of changes made by Wales head coach **Warren Gatland** for the Italy game.

749
Total metres carried by Wales over the 80 minutes in Rome.

Adam Beard sums up the mood in the camp as Wales make it two wins out of two and head for a showdown in Cardiff with England, even if he is one finger short of Wales record run of 11 wins!

Alun Wyn Jones – who came
off the bench in the second
half – addresses the troops
and focuses their minds on the
massive challenges ahead

Alun Wyn Jones gives his shorts and socks to ball boys at the end of the game

WALES V ENGLAND

Saturday 23rd February, 2019

"I knew how important this game would be.
My experience with Wales in the past is that
we always get stronger as tournaments go on.
Everyone was writing us off before so we're just
happy to come under the radar. It was probably
one of the best weeks that I've had with the
team. I knew we were right mentally."

WARREN GATLAND

No stone was left unturned in Wales' preparation to take on England – there are few bigger matches for the fans, players and management

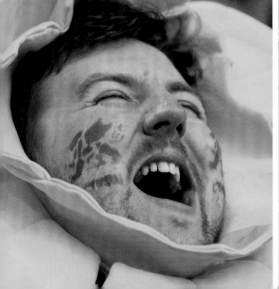

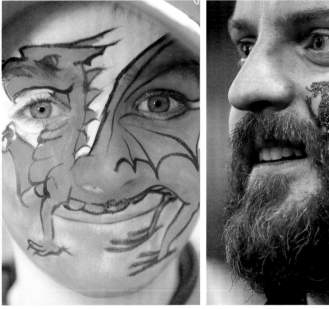

The nation is ready to
roar as Alun Wyn Jones
leads out the team

CORY HILL

The Dragons second row takes you inside the Wales camp following their historic victory

Picture the scene. We'd just beaten England, we'd had the post-match function, and we'd all boarded the bus to take us back from the Principality Stadium to our hotel, the Vale of Glamorgan.

For a brief moment there was silence – the boys were chatting, but there was not much else going on – until Shaun Edwards took control at the front of the bus. All of a sudden, this huge beat played out over the speakers and we heard: 'Dooh, dooh, dooh, Another One Bites The Dust.' Shaun had put the famous Queen song on and he was leading the charge. He's a really emotional guy, he was pumping his fist, and then it came again: 'Dooh, dooh, dooh, Another One Bites The Dust.'

The atmosphere was unbelievable. Paul 'Bobby' Stridgeon was up and down the bus. He was playing music and getting beers for everyone. He's a great guy to have around when there's a party! Bobby's a pretty special character at the best of times and he was in his element. He was blasting tunes out as well when he got the chance. The boys absolutely love him. For that bus journey I was sat next to Alan Phillips and as our team manager you don't really see him smile that often, but he told us this was the most special Wales group he's been involved in.

It struck a chord with me as Alan has been team manager since 2002! As we made our way back to the Vale he told me we would remember these times for the rest of our

lives. He's not wrong. Wales against England in Cardiff is always huge, but in many ways you don't know how big it is until you're right at the centre of it. To win was priceless for us, but we had to work very, very hard to get the victory. There was a long build-up to the game because after the France and Italy wins we had a fallow week. After a few days off we came in on the Wednesday of that week ready to go and the coaches told us to be ready for a pretty hectic 72 hours.

Warren Gatland told us we had another three or four gears in us and we knew England would be the biggest occasion of the Guinness Six Nations yet. We would have to go to another level again. We trained for three days on the bounce at the Vale in the down week and the intensity was through the roof. It's unusual for us to do that, but we certainly reaped the rewards of it.

On the Wednesday we did a big fitness test and then went straight into a full training

> **"Shaun had put the song on and was leading the charge. He's a really emotional guy, he was pumping his fist, and then it came again: 'Dooh, dooh, dooh, Another One Bites The Dust.'"**

session which is always intense anyway. That was the first time we'd done that, and then we did live contact and more running. It was seriously tough. I remember Shaun had mentioned to the boys that if we missed a tackle against England, he would feel like he'd missed one too.

We have such a tight group and as players and staff you could feel the unity, that everyone was in it together. When I look back on the campaign it maybe wasn't the most enjoyable week of training we did, but it was definitely the hardest and most rewarding. It's one we'll look back on for the rest of our days because it was where we put in all the hard work which allowed us to beat England.

Personally I was enjoying being back in Wales. Being away for the France and Italy games and training in the Nice sunshine was great, but it was also a boost to see our families again as we'd been away for a while.

I played the second half of the France game, but I didn't play in Rome because I had a cut in my kneecap. Gats made the call as there was a risk it could reopen. There was a bit of disappointment because I'd had a good run of appearances in the Wales shirt to that point.

I got picked to start against England which was a massive occasion for me. I'd been on the bench against England before in the Six Nations, but it's totally different when you start because you know you're straight into the thick of it.

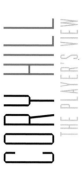
→ Growing up in Pontypridd starting against England is something I'd always dreamed of. Once we were into the week of the game training eased up a touch, but we were ready to go. I sat next to Gareth Anscombe on the bus on the way to the match. I was the line-out caller and he was playing 10 so we talked a few tactics. The bus was pretty quiet but by the time we got to St Mary Street it was a sea of red which was pretty epic. If you ask any of the boys the bus journey is always amazing but when we reached the city it was absolutely heaving. Warren doesn't tend to speak in the changing room before the game. He usually speaks to us before we leave the Vale.

For the England game we were all sat around in a huddle and Warren said to us 'England are not going to know what to expect today'. He told us we had forgotten how to lose and that we were going to win. He has an aura and he passes that on to the boys.

Warren made us believe we were going to win. We'd done all the training and we knew we could go to another level. Warren knew we would be a different animal. When he says things like that it makes you feel 10 feet tall because as a player nothing gives you more confidence than the staff around you believing in what you're doing.

Owen Farrell kicked off and the game was underway. England were 10-3 up at the break. It was calm before kick-off and it was the same at half-time. We were losing, but still pretty relaxed. We knew we hadn't fired any shots, had made a few mistakes, and hadn't really got at England. They kicked the ball a hell of a lot and we knew that was what they were going to do. Our belief was still through the roof, everyone knew we had a job to do, and we knew we'd go out in the second half and really take it to England.

I suppose the second half will always be remembered by Welshmen and women for the try I scored and then Josh Adams' score which sealed the victory. Although the game was tight, we felt we had the momentum and were the fitter side. All that training was now paying off. The try I scored after 35 phases was a huge turning point. It put us ahead for the first time and we were confident after that.

I think the ball in play time for that period was about four minutes 30-odd seconds. We prepare to play in five-minute blocks. The conditioners told us after the game that what we were doing in training was working because we were transferring it on to the field. Everyone was involved in my try. Everyone carried, rucked, or passed. It was phenomenal.

We were all absolutely knackered after 35 phases. To do that in attack is just as hard as doing it in defence. The ball went wide and all the forwards were thinking George North was going to finish it off himself. We ran over and everyone emptied the tank. Luckily for me I reacted, Dan Biggar popped it to me, and England were out on their feet as well. Harry Williams and Billy Vunipola were there in the defensive line, but there was a massive gap and like any rugby player should, I hit it. Williams went low to chop my leg and Vunipola went high. It felt like a bit of a car crash, but I just about managed to score... a moment I'll remember forever. That isn't the whole story though because as I made it over the line, I realised I'd injured my ankle at the same time!

There were 74,000 people going crazy and I was on the floor. My ankle was pretty sore, but when I realised what I'd done I jumped up and gave the crowd a clenched fist before I just about managed to stumble back to the halfway line. I got in line for the restart, Ross Moriarty caught it, but I could barely get to the next

"It was the best atmosphere of any game I've been involved in."

ruck. I remember Nicky Smith came in and tried to latch on to me, and I said 'Get off, don't touch my ankle'.

After a long kick from Dan I had to stay down then, the doctor came on, and he knew my game was over. I managed to walk off and sat down in the dugout with all the staff and strapped the ice on. I still celebrated Josh's try. I jumped about six foot in the air even with a busted ankle! It was the highest I'd jumped all game. That pretty much sealed the deal because we knew there wasn't long left. I was always going to try to get up and celebrate as it was the best atmosphere of any game I've been involved in.

After the game I wasn't thinking too much about the injury and how bad it might be. I spoke to Prav Mathema our physio and he knew my tournament was over - it was ankle ligament damage.

Prav told me these sorts of wins don't happen too often and to have a few beers, although I didn't go mad because I was in a boot and on crutches. We did enjoy the night and Warren said afterwards all our hard work had paid off, but we knew we still had two big games left and a job to do.

I had a scan on the Monday and by then I knew I wouldn't be involved in the remaining matches. It was a pretty hard time for me hearing I was going to be out of the Six Nations. When you're injured you normally leave camp straight away, but Prav spoke to Robin McBryde our forwards coach who said he'd like me to stay around and help with the line-outs. We had a leadership group with me and Adam Beard as callers and I said I would love to.

My tournament was over, but I still had a role to play off the field. Being asked to stay around to me showed the togetherness we have as a squad. I made sure there and then that I would try to help the other boys continue their search for glory in whatever way possible. ∎

The crucial try against England was Cory Hill's third in a Wales shirt

Nerves are jangling as the words of the Welsh national anthem engulf the Principality Stadium

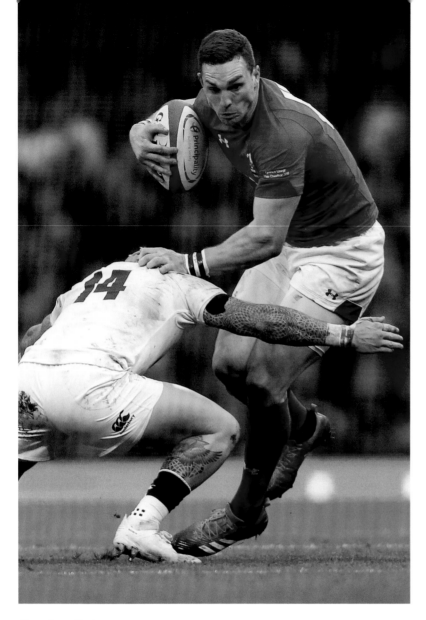

Above: George North
evades the grip of
Jack Nowell

Right: Justin Tipuric
becomes the lord of the
lineout, winning precious
first phase ball for Wales

Left: England get on the scoreboard with a try from Tom Curry

Right: Dan Biggar came off the bench and made a huge impact including a majestic crossfield kick for Josh Adams' try

Left: He's made it... Cory Hill crashes over the line after a lung-bursting 35 phases

Far left: Gareth Davies fires the ball away from a ruck

Left: Tomas Francis takes contact from two England defenders

Left: Skipper Alun Wyn Jones offloads to create space for Wales

Josh Adams acrobatically collects a kick from Dan Biggar...

... and dives over the line to confirm an incredible victory for Wales that sent a nation into raptures

Right: Josh Adams gets the party started before his team-mates join in

Opposite page: The look on the face of Jonathan Davies sums up what Adams' try means to the team and the nation

WALES 21 13 ENGLAND

Date Saturday 23rd February 2019. KO: 16.45 **Venue** Principality Stadium, Cardiff **Referee** Jaco Peyper (South Africa) **Attendance** 73,931

15 Liam Williams (Man of the Match)	**15** Elliot Daly
14 George North	**14** Jack Nowell
13 Jonathan Davies	**13** Henry Slade
12 Hadleigh Parkes (**23** Owen Watkin 80')	**12** Manu Tuilagi
11 Josh Adams	**11** Jonny May (**23** Joe Cokanasiga 70')
10 Gareth Anscombe (**22** Dan Biggar 61')	**10** Owen Farrell
9 Gareth Davies (**21** Aled Davies 77')	**9** Ben Youngs
8 Ross Moriarty (**20** Aaron Wainwright 77')	**8** Billy Vunipola
7 Justin Tipuric	**7** Tom Curry
6 Josh Navidi	**6** Mark Wilson
5 Alun Wyn Jones (Captain)	**5** George Kruis (**19** Joe Launchbury 64')
4 Cory Hill (**19** Adam Beard 71')	**4** Courtney Lawes (**20** Brad Shields 77')
3 Tomas Francis (**18** Dillon Lewis 61')	**3** Kyle Sinckler (**18** Harry Williams 57')
2 Ken Owens (**16** Elliot Dee 77')	**2** Jamie George
1 Rob Evans (**17** Nicky Smith 61')	**1** Ben Moon (**17** Ellis Genge 77')

Tries (2): Hill 68', Adams 78'	**Try:** Curry 27'
Conversion: Biggar 69'	**Conversion:** Farrell 27'
Penalties (3): Anscombe 24', 52', 57'	**Penalties (2):** Farrell 18', 63'

Scores

0-3, Farrell pen; **3-3,** Anscombe pen; **3-8,** Curry try; **3-10,** Farrell con; **6-10,** Anscombe pen; **9-10,** Anscombe pen; **9-13,** Farrell pen; **14-13,** Hill try; **16-13,** Biggar con; **21-13,** Adams try.

SIX NATIONS 2019: ROUND 3

TEAM	PL	W	D	L	PF	PA	DIFF	TF	TA	BP	PTS
Wales	3	3	0	0	71	47	24	7	5	0	12
England	3	2	0	1	89	49	40	11	5	2	10
Ireland	3	2	0	1	68	61	7	9	7	1	9
France	3	1	0	2	54	78	-24	7	10	2	6
Scotland	3	1	0	2	56	69	-13	7	10	1	5
Italy	3	0	0	3	51	85	-34	7	11	0	0

> **"We went through some pain last week in terms of the way we trained – the message to the players was there is no way anyone else is training this hard."**
>
> WARREN GATLAND

Left: Josh Adams celebrates the victory with Gareth Anscombe, both players emerging as stars in this campaign

Right: Nicky Smith shows exactly what a victory over England in Cardiff means to him

Cymru v Lloegr
23ain Chwefror 2019

Left: The achievement starts to sink in for two members of the front row union - Elliot Dee and Rob Evans

Right: Two more to go – Alun Wyn Jones addresses the squad after the third leg of the Grand Slam is achieved

3

Wales only conceded **three penalties** over the whole 80 minutes against England.

14

Number of successful tackles made by Wales captain **Alun Wyn Jones** in a monstrous display.

3

Number of points **England** were limited to in the second half at Principality Stadium.

77

Metres carried by Wales full-back and man of the match **Liam Williams**.

63

Per cent of **possession** Wales had over the course of the game.

Ross Moriarty and Gareth Anscombe take the time – with the rest of the squad – to acclaim the Wales fans

FOR THE NATION

Leading Welsh rugby author and columnist Carolyn Hitt explains why rugby is the heart and soul of the country and why this Grand Slam was so special

A lingerie shop in Bridgend might not seem the obvious place to discover what rugby means to the Welsh people but on the Monday after Wales had defeated England in the pivotal match of their 2019 Grand Slam campaign no further clues were needed. The two young female shop assistants could talk of nothing else. As I eavesdropped from the changing room, all I could hear was their detailed and passionate analysis of an "awesome" game. Only in Wales.

A quarter of an hour later, the queue for the till in Marks & Spencer was providing similar punditry. The elderly lady in front of me was dissecting the impact of the Welsh bench as the woman behind the counter folded her purchases and added her own views: "Well Biggar changed the game didn't he?"

They caught me smiling at their animated conversation. "Oh my God were you there?" And suddenly the whole queue was drawn into the chat as tales of shredded nerves, swelling choruses of Hymns & Arias and raucous celebrations were shared.

It took me back to previous situations where the grip of rugby on the nation's psyche was revealed in the most unlikely places. Like the restaurant in Llandaff a decade ago where two elegant ladies in their eighties came over to my table and said: "I hope you don't mind us disturbing you, my dear, but could you tell us: what is Gav's problem? Do you think he'll ever be back in a Welsh shirt?"

It took me even further back to my childhood against the backdrop of gods with moustaches →

→ and sideburns who dazzled and dared on the fields of play in the 1970s. "Draw a picture that means Wales to you," instructed our headmaster for the St David's Day school Eisteddfod. My friend Carol sketched a daffodil. My pal Sara penned a pithead wheel. And me? I drew Mervyn Davies.

I couldn't separate my sense of Welsh identity from 15 red shirts and an oval ball then and can't now, even if other sports can fly the flag for Wales on a global stage with similar pride. Who can forget Tour de France winner Geraint Thomas hoisting the dragon aloft on the Paris podium? And the title of Most Famous Welshman on the Planet surely goes to footballer Gareth Bale while his team-mates made an indelible impression as they reached the semi-finals of Euro 2016.

"Rugby helped create Welsh nationhood. When the game took hold in the last years of the 19th century and thrived in the first years of the 20th, Wales embraced this relatively new sport because it gave a small nation the chance to be on top of the world."

But I would argue that the way rugby is wrapped up in Welsh nationhood is unlike any other sport. Indeed, if anything rugby helped create Welsh nationhood. When the game took hold in the last years of the 19th century and thrived in the first years of the 20th, Wales embraced this relatively new sport because it gave a small nation the chance to be on top of the world.

"This is a game that came from the English public schools into Wales and became the obsession of the working class," explains historian Professor Gareth Williams. "From the 1890s we start to see big crowds, 30-40,000, the press coverage increases, people are travelling distances to watch matches and the whole club

When Wales take the field, there are 15 players on the pitch but a nation of three million right behind them

GRAND SLAM CHAMPIONS 2019

infrastructure is developing. We won the Triple Crown for the first time in 1893 and then went into the Golden Era in 1900 and won the Triple Crown six times in the next 11 years. And, of course, the great triumph, and one of the moments in the cultural history of Wales, is the victory over New Zealand in 1905." That win over the All Blacks was certainly a titanic game and one which sealed the sport in the nation's soul.

So rugby got into the bloodstream around the same time as all the other components that formed the character of industrialised Wales. "The Welsh Rugby Union becomes a national institution as part of the drive towards national bodies at the end of the 19th century," says Professor Williams. "The WRU takes its place with the National University of Wales, the National Library, the National Museum. These kinds of bodies represented the new sense of national consciousness and the WRU saw itself as very much part of that emerging national feeling."

In the 1970s, Welsh rugby enjoyed an era of glory which ensured the game became synonymous with Welshness beyond our borders. Such was the sport's hold closer to home, Gareth Edwards - the greatest player of that decade - had a statue erected in his honour in Cardiff a mere four years after he had spun his final ball from the base of the scrum.

And the 21st century has brought Wales the kind of success that still ties the game to nationhood – from the World Cup semi-final of 2011 to the Grand Slam and Six Nations championship successes of 2005, 2008, 2012 and now 2019.

This inextricable link brings a special symbiosis between spectator and player in Wales. The connection can be seen most keenly when fans and team combine to sing Hen Wlad Fy Nhadau. As Alun Wyn Jones strains every sinew on that second Gwlad, every Welsh man, woman and child is part of his team.

Hooker Ken Owens explains the bond: "Singing the anthem is special. We've got a unique anthem →

Wales fans made the pilgrimage to the Senedd in Cardiff Bay – where the National Assembly for Wales is based - to celebrate winning the Guinness Six Nations Grand Slam

"This Grand Slam has meant a lot to the Welsh people too. Each clean sweep is precious but the 2019 triumph particularly so as it marks (Warren) Gatland's Six Nations goodbye to Wales. He secured his place in history as the only coach to lead a side to this ultimate prize three times."

→ for a start. The words are different to most anthems. It's not about a monarch or battles, it's about the people and the country. So I feel it's empowering as well. When you're singing it with the thousands of people in the stadium it's their one opportunity to be at one with the players – they feel part of us instead of just being supporters like they are during the rest of the game. It's an unbelievable experience."

And each Grand Slam winner knows he is part of a bigger Welsh narrative. "The history of the jersey stretches back almost 140 years. It's never your shirt, it's the nation's jersey," says Ken. "You're only in it as a player for a certain amount of time, you cherish it and you've got to make sure you make your mark in it before you pass it on."

The red thread of the Welsh jersey is woven into us all. Ken has appreciated this from the very first time he donned it. "I'd just got into the squad when the enormity of it hit me," he smiles. "I came out of the house one morning and the binman who had never spoken to me before said 'All the best this weekend' And that was the first time I grasped what rugby meant to Welsh people - how much they care about it. It's brilliant."

This Grand Slam has meant a lot to the Welsh people too. Each clean sweep is precious but the 2019 triumph particularly so as it marks Warren Gatland's Six Nations goodbye to Wales. He secured his place in history as the only coach to lead a side to this ultimate prize three times. Gatland also accomplished something fans of my generation never thought possible – he normalised a Welsh Grand Slam. He has made something we once considered a fantasy an achievable reality. More than that even. He has made Wales expect rather than merely hope.

Wales will miss him and in a lovely speech he made during the 2019 campaign he admitted he will miss us too. "My heart will always be here," he said. Well Warren, from binmen to bra shops, from schoolkids to old ladies, there is no better place to leave your heart than in a nation that has rugby in its soul. ∎

Top right: Ken Owens appreciates exactly what the famous Wales jersey means to the players and the nation

106

FOR THE NATION

"The connection can be seen most keenly when fans and team combine to sing Hen Wlad Fy Nhadau. As Alun Wyn strains every sinew on that second Gwlad, every Welsh man, woman and child is part of his team."

Rob Evans presents the Guinness Six Nations trophy to the fans at the Senedd

SCOTLAND V WALES

Saturday 9th March, 2019

"The second half was nerve-wracking. But when you look back and have won a Grand Slam there is one game when you say 'that was a little bit lucky' ... that was definitely today. In the past we would have absorbed that pressure and cracked but at the moment we have a dream."

WARREN GATLAND

Wales arrive at BT Murrayfield, and go through meticulous preparation as they try to extend their record winning run to 13 Tests in a row

Left: Warren Gatland heads for the dressing rooms at BT Murrayfield looking for his 11th successive win as Wales coach against Scotland

Left, middle: Alun Wyn Jones (right) ensures a passionate rendition of Hen Wlad Fy Nhadau

Left, bottom: Wales fans have a special bond with their counterparts from Scotland as this has always been the Championship match where the Welsh have travelled in the biggest numbers

Right: As patron, The Princess Royal is a long-standing and committed supporter of Scottish rugby

HADLEIGH PARKES

Wales needed to find a monumental defensive performance to beat Scotland in Edinburgh and stay on course for a Grand Slam. Here is the verdict of one of the men at the centre of that red wall

SCOTLAND V WALES

'm not sure I'll ever forget the changing room after the match with Scotland. The game had been like a war, and my wife Suzy wasn't best pleased when she saw me at the full-time whistle. I had a cauliflower ear, stitches in a cut above my eye, and blood-splattered tape wrapped around my head. The perils of playing international rugby!

It was like a battle scene in the dressing room. There were six of us having stitches and five of those were down to us colliding with our own team-mates. We had taken each other out! Alun Wyn Jones was one. Jonathan Davies had a nasty cut which was seeping blood and Adam Beard was really battered and bruised. He looked awful!

Adam had to be stitched up good and proper and he ended up with what turned into a lovely black eye a few days later. The medical staff were working overtime and the boys were in pieces, but to be in a changing room like the one after the Scotland match is why I love playing rugby. It's a down-to-earth game, you go out there and play hard and fair, and then when you come back in you sit down with your mates, have a beer, and chew the fat.

As players we talked with each other and the rest of the coaches about the win, and there was a great atmosphere. It was an awesome buzz after the game.

Victory in Scotland made it four straight wins in the Guinness Six Nations and extended our winning run to 13 matches in total. It pushed us to within one game of a Grand Slam, but we didn't talk too much about that for a couple of reasons. Firstly, we were too tired and secondly, we didn't want to get too far ahead of ourselves.

We enjoyed what we'd achieved in Scotland,

> **"It was like a battle scene in the dressing room. There were six of us having stitches and five of those were down to us colliding with our own team-mates."**

but we quickly realised we had set up a Grand Slam game and those sorts of opportunities don't come around very often. You don't want to ruin those chances.

I had a picture with Suzy after the game and I looked in a right state. There was dried blood everywhere. I was thinking about what she was going to say, but my attitude was that I was already married anyway! It was too late for her!

I think the fact I had been named man of the match made my appearance a little easier on the eye! The Scotland game was extra special to me because I had my brother Scott there watching. He flew straight into Edinburgh – from New Zealand - and it was awesome to have him over. He hadn't seen me play live for about five years, but certainly saw a pretty brutal Test match.

There was a lot of red in the crowd and one of my most vivid memories of Edinburgh was the number of Welsh supporters. When we were driving into the stadium there were a huge amount of our fans there. It made us all sit up and take notice as a squad. Scotland is traditionally →

A battered and bruised Hadleigh Parkes enjoys the warm glow of victory with his family

Man of the Match, Parkes enjoyed his best game of the tournament against Scotland

→ one of the trips the Welsh fans like going to most and that was certainly the case again. Coming into the stadium to the sound of bagpipes was pretty cool and not something you get every day. Personally, I loved it! Playing in front of a full BT Murrayfield was very different to when I'd played there before against Edinburgh for the Scarlets. It's quite an eerie feeling playing in such a massive stadium with not many people there.

Going into the game we knew we were on a decent run and confidence was high after our win over England, but at the same time we weren't taking Scotland lightly at all. Fair play to Scotland. They threw everything at us and more. They forced us to dig very deep and the second half for me summed up what our environment is all about. Everyone just works so hard for each other. We all enjoy each other's company and will do anything for each other. That all came through against Scotland. We put in tackle after tackle to try and repel the home attacks.

Our defence coach Shaun Edwards is brilliant to work with. He really cares and that goes down to the players. I'm sure he would have been pleased with what he saw from us that day.

It was all about attitude and ours was fantastic. We had very little ball and to hold Scotland out for so long – I think it was about half an hour – showed great determination. I'm sure there was probably a little bit of panic among some of the boys at some points, but at the end of the day we have great belief in our system and defensive structure. The senior leadership group really stepped up in that game. It was a superb win.

When you're caught up in the middle of the game, it's all about the next moment. You have to make sure you win your individual battle. We knew we'd put in a lot of tackles, but it was only in the next few days when we did the debrief that we found out how many.

Josh Navidi and Justin Tipuric led the way in particular, but every player put their body on the

"It was all about attitude and ours was fantastic. We had very little ball and to hold Scotland out for so long – I think it was about half an hour – showed great determination."

line and we were all feeling it the next day.

Scotland did score a nice try through Darcy Graham and to their credit it was a neat move. Finn Russell was heavily involved in that and he's a fantastic player. He also kicked two penalties.

After Graham's try we just seemed to get on the wrong side of the referee. It allowed Scotland plenty of possession and territory. Thankfully we kept them out, but I was impressed with the resilience Scotland showed despite losing lots of players to injury. They had three or four guys forced off and they ended up with their scrum-

half on the wing.

We all played for each other and we'd spoken about the togetherness of the squad and playing for the whole of Wales during the build-up to the game.

It had been a very confusing week. Everyone in the squad had been made aware of the talk of a proposed merger between the Ospreys and (my region) Scarlets in the days leading up to us leaving for Edinburgh. It didn't happen in the end, but it was certainly one of the more unusual things I've had to deal with while preparing for a Test match.

The fact we had the game to focus on helped us. I'm not sure we used it as extra motivation, but our flight up to Scotland really saw us rally together. It made an already tight team spirit close to unbreakable. We were very professional and we had to put it all to one side and deliver a performance. After defending for so long, I'm sure I wasn't the only one who was delighted when we won a penalty right at the end of the game and Gareth Anscombe kicked the goal.

It had been one of my better games for Wales. I really enjoyed playing in it, I managed to get my hands on the ball a lot, and I carried hard. Gareth kept giving me possession and I just tried to get us over the gain line. I managed to get a few big hits in and it was just great to be part of a superb team performance. Man of the match could have gone to a number of people in my view, but it was nice my name was pulled out of the hat by Martyn Williams. It was just a shame I looked like I did when I had to do the television interview afterwards!

Scotland will always be a special afternoon for me. After the England game we talked about taking our chance and going on to win the Six Nations, but we knew we still had one very tough away game left. To go to Edinburgh and win to set up what was in the end a week I'll remember for the rest of my life – I'll always be grateful for being a part of it. Now there was just one more step to go. ∎

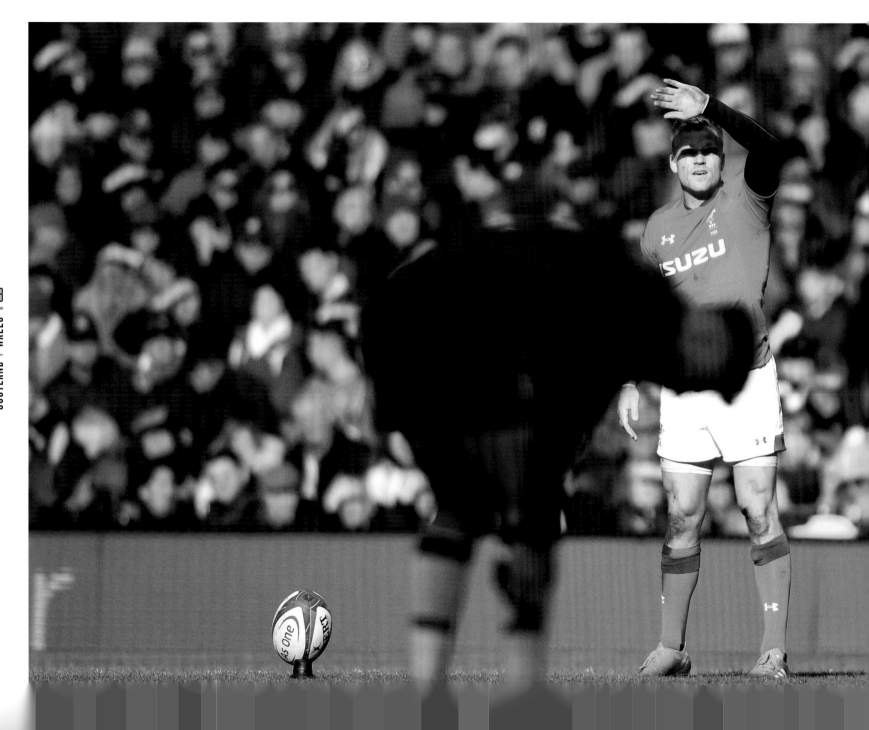

Left: Gareth Anscombe's boot was vital again as he kicked eight points

Above: When the pressure grew George North's strength in attack and in defence was an important factor out wide

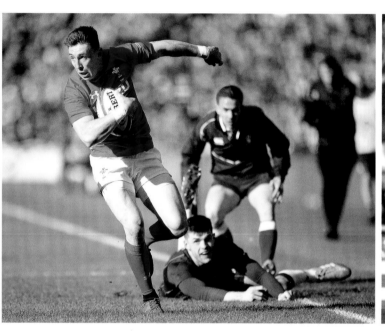

Josh Adams' route to a brilliant try for Wales

Left: Jonathan Davies' defensive effort was world-class and he was also on hand to deftly finish a long Welsh move for his try

Above: Jake Ball brought his physicality in two spells off the bench to replace Adam Beard

Left: Alun Wyn Jones'
leadership was never more
important than at BT
Murrayfield where Wales
had to dig very deep to win

Below: Justin Tipuric
(in support of Elliot Dee)
produced another
remarkable performance
with 22 tackles, missing none

SCOTLAND 11 18 WALES

Date Saturday 9th March 2019. KO: 14.15 **Venue** BT Murrayfield Stadium, Edinburgh **Referee** Pascal Gauzere (France) **Attendance** 67,144

15 Blair Kinghorn (**22** Adam Hastings 32')	**15** Liam Williams (**22** Dan Biggar 48')
114 Tommy Seymour (**23** Byron McGuigan 21')	**14** George North
13 Nick Grigg	**13** Jonathan Davies
12 Pete Horne	**12** Hadleigh Parkes (Man of the Match) (**23** Owen Watkin 74')
11 Darcy Graham (**21** Greig Laidlaw 65')	**11** Josh Adams
10 Finn Russell	**10** Gareth Anscombe
9 Ali Price	**9** Gareth Davies (**21** Aled Davies 70')
8 Josh Strauss (**20** Hamish Watson 65')	**8** Ross Moriarty
7 Jamie Ritchie (**20** Hamish Watson 9') (**16** Fraser Brown 15'-21')	**7** Justin Tipuric
6 Magnus Bradbury	**6** Josh Navidi
5 Jonny Gray (**19** Ben Toolis 65')	**5** Alun Wyn Jones (Captain)
4 Grant Gilchrist	**4** Adam Beard (**19** Jake Ball 21'-32' and 62')
3 Willem Nel (**18** Simon Berghan 65')	**3** Tomas Francis (**18** Dillon Lewis 65')
2 Stuart McInally (Captain) (**16** Fraser Brown 70')	**2** Ken Owens (**16** Elliot Dee 65')
1 Allan Dell	**1** Rob Evans (**17** Nicky Smith 62')

Try: Graham 58'	**Tries (2):** Adams 13', J Davies 30'
Penalties (2): Russell 11', 21'	**Conversion:** Anscombe 14'
	Penalties (2): Anscombe 24', 80'

Scores
3-0, Russell pen; **3-5,** Adams try; **3-7,** Anscombe con; **6-7,** Russell pen; **6-10,** Anscombe pen;
6-15, Davies try; **11-15,** Graham try; **11-18,** Anscombe pen.

Jonathan Davies shows how hard Wales had to work at BT Murrayfield to stay on course for the Grand Slam

SIX NATIONS 2019: ROUND 4

TEAM	PL	W	D	L	PF	PA	DIFF	TF	TA	TB	PTS
Wales	4	4	0	0	89	58	31	9	6	0	16
England	4	3	0	1	146	63	83	19	7	3	15
Ireland	4	3	0	1	94	75	19	13	9	2	14
Scotland	4	1	0	3	67	87	-20	8	12	2	6
France	4	1	0	3	68	104	-36	9	14	2	6
Italy	4	0	0	4	65	142	-77	9	19	0	0

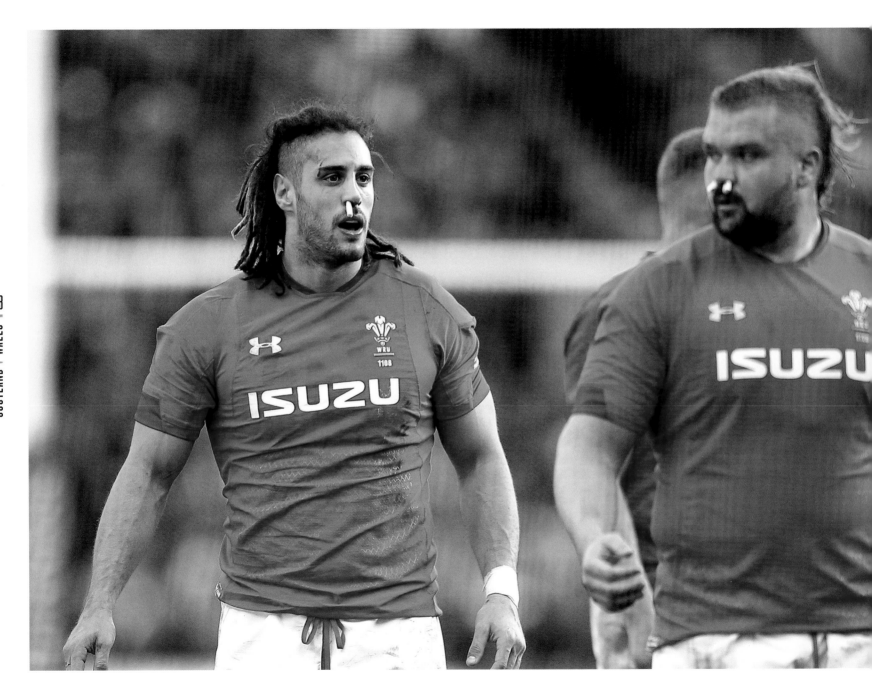

Josh Navidi, Tomas Francis and Adam Beard show the battle scars of victory against Scotland

194

Tackles made by Wales over the course of the 80 minutes in Edinburgh.

23

Number of successful tackles made by Wales flanker **Josh Navidi** at BT Murrayfield.

9

Ball carries from **Hadleigh Parkes** who was named man of the match.

42

Percentage possession Wales had to deal with.

25

Wales only enjoyed 25% possession in the second half, such was their **incredible defensive display.**

Above: Ross Moriarty emptied the tank to help Wales to a seven-point victory while Alun Wyn Jones (right) grabbed his 62nd Welsh win – a new record

WALES V IRELAND

Saturday 16th March, 2019

"These are the moments you play and live for. They are the reason you get up early to go to training, put all the hard work in, and make all the sacrifices. I wanted to enjoy it as you never know when you'll get an opportunity like that again."

GARETH ANSCOMBE

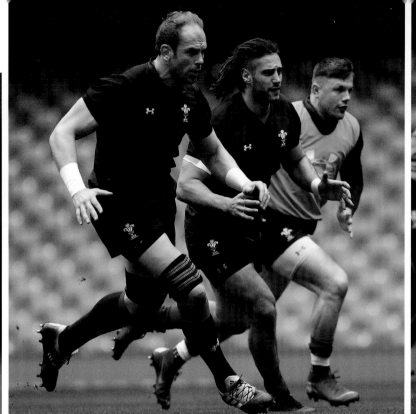

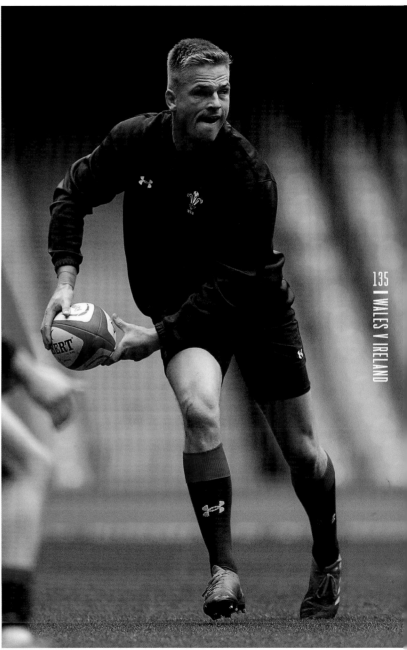

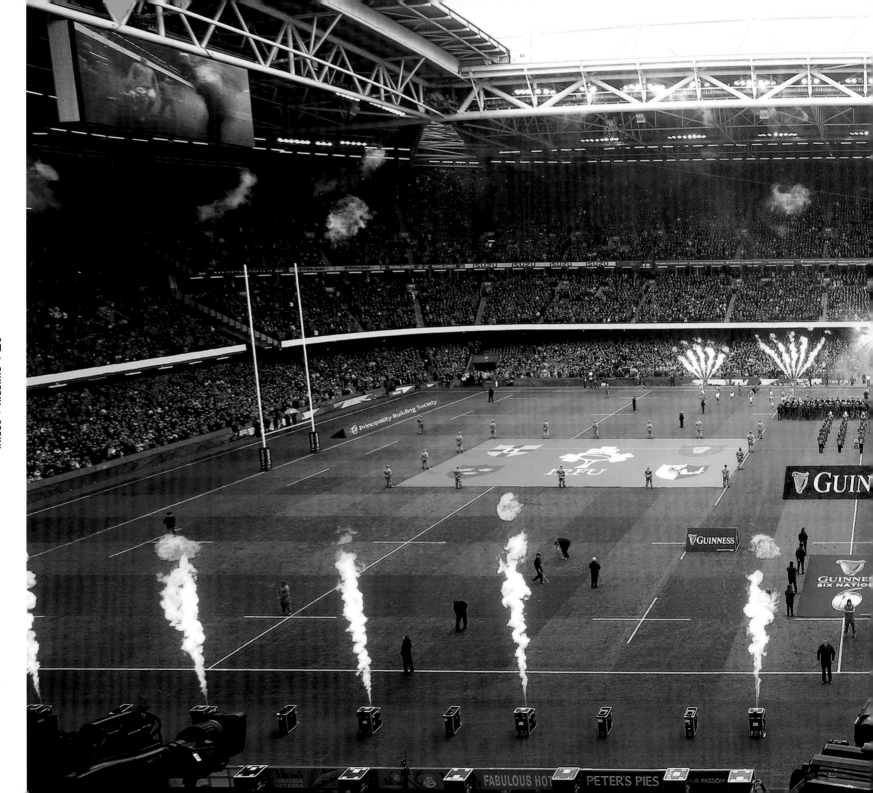

The stage is set for one of the most important matches in the recent history of Welsh rugby: the fans playing a crucial role in a historic victory

GARETH ANSCOMBE

The Wales outside-half relives one of the greatest days of his career

It was the perfect storm – Wales against Ireland in Cardiff on the final Guinness Six Nations weekend. Our first Grand Slam since 2012 and our first title since 2013 were just one win away. It doesn't get much bigger than that and we knew it. A big few days lay ahead.

Once we'd beaten Scotland, we all felt the competition was building nicely into a pretty big finale. When we met up on the Monday night I could sense very quickly there was an extra edge about the place. It was the same when we started training. I didn't go out much that week, but I heard from friends that the game was all anyone was talking about.

We couldn't go anywhere without people wishing us luck and tried to stay cool amid all the excitement. Early on in the week I remember scrolling through social media on my phone and a highlight of Gavin Henson's kick in Wales' 2005 Six Nations win over England came up. I'd seen it on the TV growing up. That is one of the biggest moments in recent Welsh rugby history and was massive in helping Wales to win that year's Grand Slam. At the time I remember looking at the kick as a kid and all I could think was how big a strike it was. Henson just struck it so cleanly. He sent the stadium into meltdown.

All those years later and with another Grand Slam on the line, it was now my turn to take a similar shot at goal. It was wide out on the right side of the Principality Stadium as we were playing, close to the tunnel. People told me afterwards it was almost identical to Henson's.

It was a tough kick early on and we weighed up whether to go for the corner, but I was confident and I had the belief I could hit it well. We were already 7-0 up and I couldn't have wished to hit it much better. I'd been working hard with Neil Jenkins over the course of the campaign. I didn't start as well as I would have liked off the tee, but I slowly grew into my kicking as the matches went by. It was nice to see that one sail between the posts. It calmed everyone down, we all took confidence from it, and everything unfolded pretty nicely for us from there. I still can't believe it.

To be a part of Welsh rugby history meant everything to me and we had a pretty good week leading up to the game. We'd won all four matches in the Six Nations and 13 in a row in total. The media had told us a lot about it being a new Welsh record, but we tried to ignore that.

The day of the game came around very quickly

> **"The Wales fans are always amazing but for the Ireland game you could just sense it was going to be something different."**

and with it being a relatively early kick-off, we were soon on the bus from our hotel in the Vale of Glamorgan to the Principality Stadium.

The Wales fans are always amazing and our journey to the ground is always a special trip, but for the Ireland game, you could just sense it was going to be something different. There were lots more people than usual, but it was more than that. You could almost sense something special was going to happen that day. As soon as we got to Pontcanna the whole place was packed and the last bit of the bus journey certainly took a bit longer than usual. As we came into the city and slowed down to get into the stadium it was a pretty cool experience. There were a lot of fans waiting for us to come in, they were making a lot of noise, and the chants had already started. It all made the hairs on the back of my neck stand up and as soon as we started warming up, the crowd started singing.

Fast forward a few hours and with 10 minutes to go we knew the game was in the bag. It was nice to be on the field then and take it all in. It was definitely much better than being anxious about holding on to try and get the result! I remember when there was a stoppage in play late on I just took a moment, looked around the stadium, and heard the supporters chanting.

These are the moments you play and live for. They are the reason you get up early to go to training, put all the hard work in, and make all the

→ sacrifices. I wanted to enjoy it as you never know when you'll get an opportunity like that again.

We trained pretty well throughout the week and as we got closer to the game there was the debate about whether the roof was going to be open or closed. To me that just added to the intrigue. In the end the roof was open and the forecast rain soon arrived during the warm-ups. We had prepared for it to be wet and miserable. We wanted to start well and to try to build a lead. In those sorts of conditions any lead you get is priceless and we couldn't have wished for a better first half.

From the kick-off George North tackled Jacob Stockdale straight into touch, we won an early line-out, and Hadleigh Parkes' try was a great way for us to settle and to get the crowd into the game. We had spoken about some option-taking when we had penalty advantages and not always kicking the ball away. I knew we had a bit of a free play and from the work we had done all week, we thought we could find some kicking space with the way Ireland defend as a back three. I chipped the ball ahead and Hadleigh did the rest with less than two minutes played. Dream start! The wet weather made for difficult kicking conditions, but I managed to convert the try and add three more penalties for a 16-0 half-time lead.

Hadleigh's tackle on Stockdale as he raced clear earlier was a big moment. We were in control but we also knew we'd come from 16-0 down in the first game in France. There was no way we were going to be taking the second half lightly.

By that stage I had moved to full-back with Dan Biggar coming on after an injury to George, but when we restarted I kicked two more penalties and it felt like everything was going to go our way after that. The crowd had been immense all day, but they really got into it in the second half and when they get involved, we're a hard team to beat. I talked to Ireland head coach Joe Schmidt after the game and he said that with the conditions getting wetter and wetter, each

penalty we kicked was almost worth six rather than three because it was so hard to get back into the game with a greasy ball. It made it difficult to play with ball in hand. With every kick being so important, it was nice for me to end with seven from seven.

Ireland scored right at the end and we were disappointed to concede which just shows how high our standards are. Still, it wasn't going to ruin our party! To walk around the field after the final whistle was just amazing. It had rained all day and 40 minutes after the final whistle the fans were still there. It was brilliant to share that emotion with them and give them something to celebrate.

I've been lucky enough to have had some great moments in my career and won a couple of trophies, but the fact the Ireland game was at home and we knew how much it meant both to us and the entire nation means it will be pretty tough to top.

People always ask me now what the celebrations were like afterwards. The fact I had my family and friends there in the crowd made it extra special. I spoke to my parents Mark and Tracy straight after the Scotland match and we made the call they had to be there for Ireland. They flew straight over from New Zealand. We'd have been kicking ourselves if they hadn't made it. My fiancée Milica and two of my best mates from London were also there.

I was proud to be named man of the match and the cheer I got when I was doing my TV interview afterwards is something I'll always remember.

> **"The crowd had been immense all day, but they really got into it in the second half and when they get involved, we're a hard team to beat."**

Once we'd lifted the Guinness Six Nations and Triple Crown trophies and done a lap of the field, there was a lot of champagne being sprayed around in the changing room. We certainly took some time to be in that moment. We made sure we didn't get changed too quickly, we had a beer and a chat with everyone, sang a few songs, and just jumped around. Those are the moments I will really miss when I stop playing the game.

Prince William was there too. I'd met him before at the Rugby World Cup. He's a lovely guy and it's just remarkable when he talks to you because he knows your name! I always find that amazing. He was really chuffed for us and enjoyed sharing the moment in the changing room. We had a few photos and a chat. It's when you're having a beer with a prince that you really have to pinch yourself! It was a lot of fun in the changing rooms and we enjoyed the moment, but Warren Gatland was pretty grounded. He was just delighted we'd ticked another box on our journey.

The next 48 hours is pretty hazy! Liam Williams organises the after-party events. He sorted out a few things for us after the game. Rob Evans is another who is always the life and soul of the party and we went into Cardiff with our other halves. We made sure we celebrated hard that's for sure and on the Sunday we got together again and had a few more beers. We had a parade down at the Senedd in Cardiff Bay on the Monday. It was great to share that moment with so many supporters. After that the hangover started to kick in and we slowly returned to normality, but the memories of the 2019 Six Nations will last a lifetime.

Whenever we meet up as a Wales squad we want to end the campaign with silverware. We've managed to do it in the last few campaigns, we're on a terrific run at the moment, but now the focus has turned to the Rugby World Cup. It will take a lot of hard work, but we're pretty confident we can go to Japan and do something pretty special. We'll need an ounce of luck for sure, but our aim is to make the country proud once again. ■

Anscombe was pivotal in
helping Wales to their third
Grand Slam under Head
Coach Warren Gatland

Above: Anscombe slots another kick on the day he contributed 20 points to the Wales win

Right: The red wall was crucial in this win, Wales putting in 177 tackles, compared to 87 by Ireland

Hadleigh Parkes gave Wales the dream start with a try in the second minute (left) which clearly meant so much to him (above)

Left: There was no way through for Rob Kearney as Wales kept Ireland try-less until the final minute

Above: George North suffered early agony after being a key player in the Grand Slam campaign

Left: Alun Wyn Jones battled through injury to lead Wales to victory in the final match

Left: Ken Owens turned in another world-class performance, helping the Wales scrum get the edge

Above: Dan Biggar, Nicky Smith and Jake Ball come up with the perfect plan to foil Ireland

Above: Josh Adams clears in heavy Irish traffic

Right: Captain Alun Wyn Jones proved himself to be one of Wales' greatest leaders in this campaign

The Wales defence put Johnny Sexton under extreme pressure in Cardiff

WALES 25 7 IRELAND

Date Saturday 16th March 2019. KO: 14.45 **Venue** Principality Stadium, Cardiff **Referee** Angus Gardner (Australia) **Attendance** 74,500

Wales	Ireland
15 Liam Williams	**15** Rob Kearney (**23** Jordan Larmour 65')
14 George North (**22** Dan Biggar 9')	**14** Keith Earls
13 Jonathan Davies	**13** Garry Ringrose
12 Hadleigh Parkes (**23** Owen Watkin 71')	**12** Bundee Aki
11 Josh Adams	**11** Jacob Stockdale
10 Gareth Anscombe (Man of the Match)	**10** Jonathan Sexton (**22** Jack Carty 72')
9 Gareth Davies (**21** Aled Davies 57')	**9** Conor Murray (**21** Kieran Marmion 67')
8 Ross Moriarty (**20** Aaron Wainwright 71')	**8** CJ Stander
7 Justin Tipuric	**7** Seán O'Brien (**20** Jack Conan 52')
6 Josh Navidi	**6** Peter O'Mahony
5 Alun Wyn Jones (Captain)	**5** James Ryan
4 Adam Beard (**19** Jake Ball 71')	**4** Tadhg Beirne (**19** Quinn Roux 59')
3 Tomas Francis (**18** Dillon Lewis 54')	**3** Tadhg Furlong (**18** Andrew Porter 65')
2 Ken Owens (**16** Elliott Dee 61')	**2** Rory Best (Captain) (**16** Niall Scannell 65')
1 Rob Evans (**17** Nicky Smith 54')	**1** Cian Healy (**17** David Kilcoyne 59')

Try: Parkes 2'

Conversion: Anscombe 3'

Penalties (6): Anscombe 18', 36', 40', 49', 54', 70'

Try: Larmour 80'

Conversion: Carty 81'

Scores
5-0, Parkes try; **7-0,** Anscombe con; **10-0,** Anscombe pen; **13-0,** Anscombe pen; **16-0,** Anscombe pen; **19-0,** Anscombe pen; **22-0,** Anscombe pen; **25-0,** Anscombe pen; **25-5,** Larmour try; **25-7,** Carty con.

SIX NATIONS 2019: ROUND 5

TEAM	PL	W	D	L	PF	PA	DIFF	TF	TA	TB	PTS
Wales	5	5	0	0	114	65	49	10	7	0	23
England	5	3	1	1	184	101	83	24	13	4	18
Ireland	5	3	0	2	101	100	1	14	10	2	14
France	5	2	0	3	93	118	-25	12	15	1	10
Scotland	5	1	1	3	105	125	-20	14	17	2	9
Italy	5	0	0	5	79	167	-88	10	22	0	0

Alun Wyn Jones became part of an exclusive band of Welshmen to win three Grand Slams

THE BREAKDOWN

3
Victory over Ireland made Wales boss **Warren Gatland** the only head coach in Six Nations history to win three Grand Slams.

20
Total points scored by man of the match **Gareth Anscombe** for Wales.

19
Number of **dominant tackles** made by Wales, summing up their desire. Ireland made just six.

80
Minutes Wales went without conceding before **Jordan Larmour** scored right at the death for Ireland.

3
Alun Wyn Jones captained Wales to victory and joined a select band of Welshman on three Grand Slams after a monumental display.

Adam Beard and Nicky Smith can hardly believe they are Grand Slam winners

"I'm so proud of all the players and the backroom staff. Anything can happen when you are a proud nation and work hard and we've done that over the last nine weeks"

ALUN WYN JONES, THE ONLY SURVIVOR OF WARREN GATLAND'S FIRST SLAM

Cymru v Iwerddon
16eg Mawrth 2019

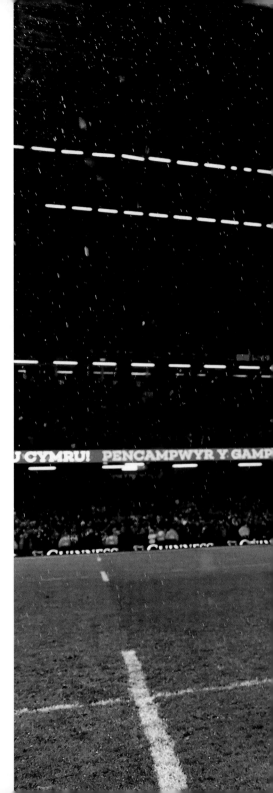

Liam Williams is ecstatic
as he becomes a Grand
Slam winner

Far right: Josh Adams
jumps for joy as the young
wing realises he has
helped make rugby history

Far left: Jonathan Davies emerged from the 2019 campaign as one of the world's best players

Left: The two Grand Slam skippers – Jonathan Davies and Alun Wyn Jones enjoy a special moment at the end of the match

CHAMPIONS!

2019 Guinness Six Nations & Grand Slam Winners

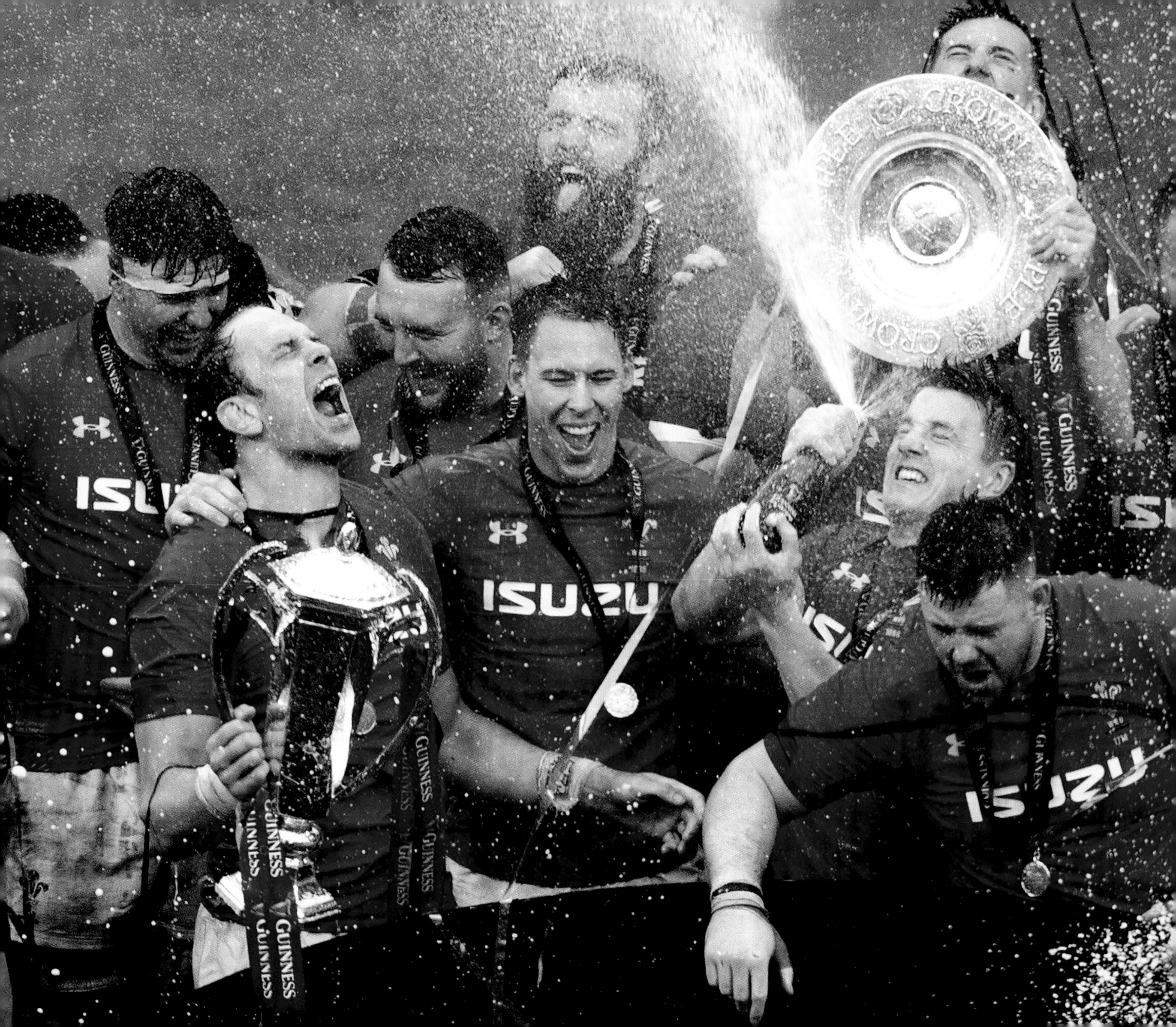
ISUZU
ISUZU
ISUZU
GUINNESS
GUINNESS
GUINNESS

Above: The look on the face of Alun Wyn Jones says it all – Wales are the champions

Left: Jonathan Davies, Dan Biggar, Rob Evans, Hadleigh Parkes and Gareth Davies are loving life as Grand Slam winners

Opposite page: The team lift the Guinness Six Nations trophy and it starts to sink in that they have made history

Above: Baggage Master John Rowlands enjoys a precious moment on the pitch with members of his family

Above, right: Personal Assistant to the Wales National Squad Caroline Morgan joins the party

Right: It's all smiles for kicking guru Neil Jenkins and Strength & Conditioning Coach Huw Bennett

Far right: Attack Coach Rob Howley was pivotal to Wales' Grand Slam win

Opposite page: The two Six Nations captains - Jonathan Davies and Alun Wyn Jones - take the acclaim of the nation

Above: Josh Navidi emerged as a truly world-class player in 2019

Above, centre: All the hard work is worth it for Nicky Smith, Adam Beard, Justin Tipuric and Owen Watkin

Above, right: Cory Hill and Neil Jenkins are all smiles

Right: Ken Owens displays the Guinness Six Nations trophy and the Triple Crown on the lap of honour

Far right: Dillon Lewis' dreams come true with that precious medal

The smiles on the faces of Gareth Anscombe and the supporters tell the story

Elliot Dee, Dillon Lewis and Rob Evans finally get their hands on the trophies every player wants

Far left: Sports Scientist Ryan Chambers gets his teeth stuck in to the silverware

Left: Performance Analysts Gwern James, Andy Hughes, Rhodri Bown and Marc Kinnaird see the fruits of their labour translated into trophies

Below, left: The team's National Medical Manager Prav Mathema gets fired up

Below, centre: A special moment for Soft Tissue Therapists Angela Rickard and Hanlie Fouche

Below: Team Manager Alan Phillips was a vital cog in the team's Grand Slam success

Above: Liam Williams and Hadleigh Parkes share a joke with Prince William

Left: Paul Stridgeon takes the chance for a Royal Grand Slam selfie

Head Coach Warren Gatland stands proudly with the Guinness Six Nations trophy

HOW THE 2019 GRAND SLAM WAS WON

By Warren Gatland

"If we win in Paris, I think we can win the Six Nations". It was a quote that raised a few eyebrows to say the least! I first mentioned it on stage at a private dinner for the Rugby Union Writers' Club and followed it up on the record a week or so later at the Guinness Six Nations media launch in London where the writers could put it into print properly!

Why did I say it? For a couple of reasons. Firstly, the Six Nations is all about momentum and building it throughout the tournament. With the way our fixtures fell this year we knew a huge game in Paris first up on a Friday night would be crucial. We knew if we won there it would get the ball rolling. With the games against England and Ireland in Cardiff you have to back yourself and I believed that getting the victory against France would kick-off our tournament and from there the momentum would follow.

Secondly, it was an important message. It was a message that may have got picked up by our players and by the opposition. If our players hear me say that and hear me believe it, hopefully they would too.

At half-time in the rain at the Stade de France it wasn't about momentum, it was about us getting ourselves back into the game. We spoke before the match about dominating, playing the conditions, and taking the first couple of weeks of training – which had been pretty hellish for the players – out on to the pitch.

"With the games against England and Ireland in Cardiff you have to back yourself and I believed that getting the victory against France would kick-off our tournament."

The first 40 minutes of our campaign didn't go to plan. France started the better, managed the conditions better than we did, got on the front-foot, and deserved their half-time lead.

There wasn't screaming or shouting at half-time, no rollicking from the coaches. As a squad we simply went through what we needed to do and how we needed to execute the game plan and play the conditions better. We needed to believe in what we do.

We went into the match on a winning streak of nine. We hadn't become a bad team overnight and that was the message.

In the second half it was a different performance from us. It was far more composed. We had some luck along the way, but that's sport. You have to create a bit of luck and take it when it comes, but the players put in one hell of a 40 minutes and got the win to start the ball rolling. It wasn't something we knew until post-match, but the comeback was the biggest in Six Nations →

"I was heavily criticised in 2018 for making 10 changes against Italy. It wasn't anything to do with a lack of respect for our opponents, but a sign of respect to our squad and the players who deserve the opportunity."

→ history. There was a very well deserved pat on the back as we headed to Nice.

With back-to-back away games on the continent we felt it was a good opportunity to keep the squad together and have a training camp en-route to Rome rather than return to Cardiff. The camp would allow us to stick together as a squad, get some more time on the field and looking longer term, replicate our plans for the Rugby World Cup. It was a win-win, plus the weather was pretty decent too!

A big training week in Nice, with the daily sea recovery and the odd coffee stop, led us nicely into Italy.

I was heavily criticised in 2018 for making 10 changes against Italy. It wasn't anything to do with a lack of respect for our opponents, but a sign of respect to our squad and the players who deserved an opportunity. We ran up a big victory that year and once again we decided to make a similar number of changes. Having travelled with a squad of 31, the players who started in Rome deserved a chance and we backed them to go out there and do a job.

We all know how difficult the Italians can be in Rome. With the crowd behind them they are extremely passionate and they put in a big display on the day, but we kept calm, kept our cool, and got the job done.

Two wins from two. The momentum continued.

Following Italy we had two weeks preparation for the clash against England. That is great on the field; more time to work together and to get extra fitness into the boys (they certainly got that – they were worked extremely hard in that down week) and simply more time to prepare. Off the field, the story is quite different. The extra week just adds to the anticipation, excitement and merry go round that is Wales against England. It captures the public's and the press' attention like no other match.

We just had to go about our job like we would with any other game and ignore the distractions, the extra column inches, and the extra fuss.

Come game day that excitement hits fever pitch in Cardiff. The bus ride into the stadium is pretty special. Match day in Cardiff is unique, but it was another level that afternoon. Plenty of England supporters were out in full voice as the bus came up Westgate Street, but they were soon swamped by the sea of red which descended around the bus. It is one hell of an entrance into the stadium and one we thrive on.

To the game itself. It was what it was billed as – a huge contest. The first half was hugely physical with both sides going at it and England edging in front with the only try of the first 40.

Again, half-time was simply about just re-iterating the message of us needing to do what we do and believing what we could do. As the players went back out behind on the score sheet, we truly believed a third victory would be in our grasp. We controlled that second half, upped the tempo and the physicality, and showed our true self. Cory's (Hill) try came off a massive effort. The control and patience we showed was fantastic and it was rounded off with a great score to take us into the lead.

From that try we continued to push, both in attack and defence, and sealed the match with Josh Adams taking a great high ball out wide to score. The atmosphere was already electric in the stadium and Josh's try would have surely →

Top: It all started with a spectacular come-from-behind 24-19 victory in Paris

Above, right: The French win was followed by a 26-15 success for a much-changed side in Rome

Right, and top right: The nation began to believe the Grand Slam was on after the 21-13 triumph over England

Centre, far right: Wales' fourth victory also came on the road, at BT Murrayfield, 18-11

Bottom, far right: Wales finally got their hands on the Grand Slam after a comprehensive 25-7 win over Ireland

"You are involved in professional sport to experience days like that and we have been pretty lucky to experience a few of them."

Above, left: The boss embraces Ken Owens after victory over Ireland was sealed

Above, middle: The smile says it all... Wales are the champions

Above, right: We catch a glimpse of the unsung heroes in the coaching team

Opposite page: The dressing room after the win over Ireland is a happy place as the Wales players and coaches reflect on a job well done

→ raised the roof... had it been closed that day!

Three from three. Now people start believing!

We faced another down week before travelling up to Scotland. Again we went through what we needed to do in camp with the boys recovering from the previous weekend whilst focusing on the tie up in Edinburgh. We had to ensure the right message was out in the press and the public. Some people externally were already talking a Grand Slam decider and talking about the finale against Ireland. We weren't thinking that at all and were keen for that internal message to be replicated externally.

Our games up in Scotland always have a cracking atmosphere and our hosts, whilst looking to right a few wrongs from the opening matches in this year's tournament, would have been confident following their victory over Wales a couple of years back at BT Murrayfield.

Like two years ago we dominated the first 40 and we were in complete control at the break.

Scotland again fought back and produced a big second half. We had to defend like our lives depended on it. We certainly did that and rose to the task. It was a huge effort once again to claim victory. At full time history hadn't repeated itself, we were 4/4, and I was still unbeaten against Scotland as Wales coach. Now we could talk about Ireland!

Grand Slam week and it's pretty exciting inside and outside of camp. Ireland were coming to Cardiff as defending champions and were still in with a chance of the title themselves. It was all teed up for a huge super Saturday and it didn't disappoint.

Emotion plays a huge part in big Test matches and it did on that day. Our players knew we were playing for first or third. We knew what was riding on the match, what was at stake, and with a big, passionate support behind us, the game built and built.

From the early try we were dominant and continued to push and push. The players got exactly what they deserved – not only the win, but the title and the Grand Slam. It made it 14

wins on the bounce.

Post match was pretty special, pretty emotional, and you have to soak up the atmosphere. We were soaked on the pitch as the rain fell, but that really didn't matter. The players had just created history again. No-one can take records or trophies away from you and the players thoroughly deserved the title.

You are involved in professional sport to experience days like that and we have been pretty lucky to experience a few of them.

For me it was my last Six Nations game with Wales and the perfect way to end it even more so being at home in Cardiff. I will miss match days in Cardiff, the full house of the stadium, the journey in on the bus, the fans, and the celebrations afterwards. It all makes it so special.

The players worked their rear ends off in this campaign and we pushed them extremely hard. Putting the red jersey on means everything to our players, they are extremely proud to play for their country, and I'm hugely proud of the squad and what we have achieved. ■

ROLL OF HONOUR

Congratulations to the Wales team for their Grand Slam success

Forwards:
Jake Ball
Adam Beard
Leon Brown
Seb Davies
Elliot Dee
Ryan Elias
Rob Evans
Tomas Francis
Cory Hill
Alun Wyn Jones (Capt.)
Wyn Jones
Samson Lee
Dillon Lewis
Ross Moriarty
Josh Navidi
Ken Owens
Nicky Smith
Justin Tipuric

Josh Turnbull
Aaron Wainwright
Thomas Young

Backs:
Josh Adams
Hallam Amos
Gareth Anscombe
Dan Biggar
Aled Davies
Gareth Davies
Jonathan Davies
Steffan Evans
Jarrod Evans
Leigh Halfpenny
Jonah Holmes
George North
Rhys Patchell
Hadleigh Parkes
Owen Watkin
Liam Williams
Scott Williams
Tomos Williams

And to the management for driving the squad to victory in the 2019 Guinness Six Nations

Management:
Warren Gatland
Shaun Edwards
Rob Howley
Neil Jenkins
Robin McBryde
Alan Phillips
Caroline Morgan
John Rowlands
Luke Broadley
Prav Mathema
Dr Geoff Davies

John Miles
Angela Rickard
Hanlie Fouche
Paul Stridgeon
Huw Bennett
Ryan Chambers
John Ashby
Jon Williams
Rhodri Bown
Andrew Hughes
Marc Kinnaird
Andre Moore

Many thanks to the following for supporting this book (and the Wales team!)

Daffyd Alderman
Tim Atkin
Kirsty Atkinson
Tracy & Steve Bates
Paul Batho
Julian Beames
Michael Bennett
Tony Bentham
Martin Bevan
Jeremy Bishop
Ciaran Blakemore
Richard Bowden
David Boyes
Matthew Brace
Ann Braiden
Brian A Brennan
Neil Brindley
Delyth Brown
Arwel Buckland
Jack Bunyan
Simon Cahill
Helen Calley
David Calton
Jose Antonio Canalo
Simon Capron
Dave Chamberlain
Philip Chan

Norman Chenery
Ken Cheung
Les Clarke
Nigel Clarke
Ferg Clemas-Howard
Julian Clemas-Howard
Annalise Coady
Nichola Collier
Stuart Collins
Evan Constance
Rhys Constance
Gerald Crocker
Emma Crooke
Haydn Cullen Jones
Stephen Culverwell
Bernice Daly
Rhodri Davey
Cristian Davies
Diane Davies
Ian V Davies
Jonathon Davies
Phil Davies
Wayne Davies
Joanne Crocker Davis
Sam Davis
Tom Dean
Paul Dixon

ROLL OF HONOUR

ROLL OF HONOUR

Sara Dodd
The Dowding Family
Richard Duke
Simon Durkin
Charlie Edwards
Chris Edwards
David Edwards
David Edwards
Thomas Edwards
Sam Etheridge
Catherine Evans
David Evans
Gwilym Evans
Ian Philpot Evans
Keith Evans
Mike Evans
Mike Evans
Tim Evans
Jordan Everley

Mike Everley
James Falvey
Tony Fardy & Family
Steve Fenn
Frances Filippi
Keith Fisher
Caitlin Fitzgerald
Keith Fitzgerald
Colin Fletcher
Steve Foster
Robert Fowler
Robert Fowler
Nigel Gibbs
Sidney Gill
Matthew Gray
Paul Gray
Marilyn Green
Adrian Griffiths
Colin Griffiths
Gareth Griffiths
Martin Griffiths
Richard Griffiths
Susan Griffiths
Ann Griffiths
Thom Griffiths
Tomos Rhys Guard
Aiden Sion Gumn
Ben Hackett
Thomas Hadley
Andrew Haigh
Darren Hamer
Dan Hancock
Alex Hancox
Tom Hanna
Codie Hardaway

Alex Harding
Lewis Harrison
David Hepworth-Sims
Jenny Higgins
Jonathan Hill
David Hitchings
Tim Hooper
Mark Horner
Aled Hughes
David Hughes
Steve Hughes
Gwyn Humphreys
Derrick Hunt
Steve Ingham
Sevi Inwood
Joel Jackson
Nathan Jackson
Alwena James
Euan A James
Hadyn A James
Ivor James
Kaye James
Rhys James
Chris Jeacott
Ann Jenkins
Tony Jenkins
Jack Waving Johnsey
Adrian Jones
Alun Jones
Cian Jones
Darren Paul Jones
Dave Jones
David Jones
Dylan Jones
Emma L Jones

Henry Jones
John Jones
Liz Melons Jones
Martyn V Jones
Michael Jones
Rhodri Jones
Rhys Jones
Robin Jones
Ruth Lewis Jones
Ryan SE Jones
Sarah Jayne Jones
Stephen Jones
Taff Jones
Tomos R V Jones
Glyn Jordan
Joanne Kemp Thomas
IHB Knights
Matthew Knott
James Lalley
Maisie Latimer
Llewellyn Layton
Stephen Leach
Andrew Lee
Ian Leeder
Chris Leigh

Jon Leonard
Alan Lewis
Graham Lewis
John Lewis
Jon Lewis
Owen Littlejohns
Lilly Ann Llewelyn
Gareth Luke
Evan Lewis Maitre
Gary Marsh
Morfydd Marsh
Gavin Marshall
Ron Marshall
Rob Biff Mathias
Robert Millett
Paula Milton
Terry Milton
Christine Morgan
Cortney Moriarty
Jonny Morris
Brian Mullen
Will Mullen
Stuart Munro
Jenny Murray
Malcolm John Neate

Craig Neen
Howard Nicholls
Hugh of Monmouth
Sarah Oliver
Gwyn Owen
Mark Owen
Mark Owen
Tim Owens
Nigel Paget
Wes Palmer
Karl Parminter
John & Jan Parry
Sian Perrin
Jac PetcJones
Mark Peters
Nigel Phillips
William Pitt
Eddie Plenty
Charlie Power
Andrew Price
David Lynne Prickett
Andy Pritchard
Gary Pritchard
Rayson Pritchard
Steven John Pritchard
Jason Mark Prosser
Rachel Ann Prosser
Mathew Pryce
Jill Ramsay
Aled Minton Rees
Wayne Rees
Jamie Rees Winter
Lily Mae Richards
Andy Roberts
Dave Roberts

Sian Roberts
Simon Roberts
Cerys Rogers
Vincent Rose
Adrian Rowlands
Richard Rowlands
Cath & Oli Ryder
John Adrian Samuel
Claudio Schmucki
Tony Schofield
Thomas Schumann
Christopher Scragg
Katherine Secombe
Darran Seho
May Ling Seho Evans
Simon Shakeshaft
Matt Smallbones
Gary Smith
Mike Smith
Paul Solomons
Alex Souter
Charlotte Steel
David Steel
Gareth Stephens

Hedley Stephenson
Stephen Steven
James Stock
Elizabeth Stone Mum
Alan Strange
Jennie Sumner
Luke Sutton
Jeffrey Tavender
The Taylor Family
Don Thomas
Geraint Thomas
Paul Thomas
Philip Glyn Thomas
TJET Thomas
William Thomas
William Thomas
Peter Thompson
Kim Tillott
Hayley Tilston
Nathaniel Titley
Ian Townsend
David Trimm
Andy Trotman
Holger True

Sonia Turley
Paolo Varini
Bethan Lowri Wainfur
Freddie Warren
Kevin Warren
Iwan Waters
Roger Watson
Adrian Welham
Ben White
Alun Williams
Gareth Williams
Jeremy Williams
Martin Williams
Matt Williams
Paul Williams
Paul Williams
Peter Williams
Rhys Williams
Richard DC Williams
William Williams
Ted Wolfenden
Lynn Wood
Ken Woodland
Richard Worsley

Acknowledgements

The Welsh Rugby Union would like to thank all those involved in producing *On To Glory!*

It is a fantastic showcase of our **2019 Guinness Six Nations Grand Slam** triumph and a keepsake for players, management and supporters alike.

To the **players** and **management**, thank you. Thank you for delivering yet another Championship and Grand Slam to Wales and for putting smiles on the face of the nation.

To our **supporters**, thank you for every cheer, every song and every ounce of your support.

Vision Sports Publishing would like to thank the following for their help:

The **players, coaches** and **backroom staff** of the **Welsh national squad** for their successful and hard-earned Guinness Six Nations campaign. Congratulations on your wonderful achievements and we hope this book does justice to them. In particular we'd like to thank those players and coaches who gave up their free time to be interviewed.

Luke Broadley, Craig Maxwell, Rhys Williams, Anna Chapman and everyone at the WRU who has worked so hard on this project and **Fanatics** for their support.

The dedicated and talented team who have put the book together: **Alex Bywater, David** at **David Hicks Design,** and the **Huw Evans Agency** - in particular, photographers **Ben Evans, Chris Fairweather, Gareth Everett, Mark Lewis** and **Aled Llywelyn.**

And finally, the **Welsh supporters.** Your passion for the team and for the sport inspires us all.

Ymlaen Cymru